The TOTAL Volunteering Book

"*The Total Volunteering Book* is a 'must-have' for anyone encouraging volunteering or thinking of doing it themselves."
Don Rowe
Director, Curriculum Resources, The Citizenship Foundation

"This neat and well-presented guide to volunteering is a timely addition to the literature of the 'giving age'. It is practical, hands-on and accessible… the listed websites will prove very helpful."
John Potter
Director, CSV Education for Citizenship

"A very comprehensive source of information. It should prove an essential reference book for schools, colleges and career services."
Christopher Spence
Chief Executive, The National Centre for Volunteering

"Very inspiring and motivating, covering a huge range of opportunities."
Mel Jones, Kids' Clubs Network

About the authors
Sandra Cain and Michelle Maxwell both have a wealth of experience in training and managing volunteers. Sandra Cain is a former grant assessor for the National Lottery Charities Board and was co-ordinator of a national charity for seven years. The authors were the co-founders of the Communication Development Trust, a voluntary organization which provides training and development within the voluntary sector.

Get a Life!

The TOTAL Volunteering Book

Sandra Cain & Michelle Maxwell

Illustrated by Polly Dunbar

A & C BLACK • LONDON

First published in 2001 by A & C Black (Publishers) Ltd
35 Bedford Row
London
WCIR 4JH

ISBN 0-7136-5315-9

Photographic credits
The authors and publishers are grateful for permission to reproduce the following photographs:
Cover: (left) supplied by the National Centre for Volunteering; (right) Alex Livesey/Allsport; page 8: Lawrence Lustig; page 19: supplied by the NSPCC; page 21: supplied by UNICEF.

Acknowledgements
The authors would like to thank Bournemouth Helping Services, the pupils of the Blandford School, the Institute for Volunteering Research and all the inspiring young volunteers for their help in the research and writing of this book.

Neither the authors nor the publishers can accept legal responsibility for any errors or omissions in the information contained in this book. Potential volunteers should check all information with the organizations in whose work they are interested.

A CIP catalogue record for this book is available from the British Library.

Printed and bound in Great Britain by
Creative Print and Design (Wales), Ebbw Vale

CONTENTS

Part 2: The word on the street

Part 3: The directory

Part 4: What next?

foreword

"Volunteering is a great way to pledge support for an individual or organization. Many organizations which are doing excellent work for the community rely on the goodwill of individuals who are thoughtful enough to give up their spare time.

At some stage of their lives, many youngsters and older people alike may need the support of someone outside the family. Often that other person, whether at the end of a phone line or in person, is working as a volunteer."

Lennox Lewis MBE

World Boxing Heavyweight Champion
and British Sports Personality of the Year 1999

About this book

This book will help you find out everything you need to know about volunteering – what it is, why lots of people do it and how you can get involved. It's packed with loads of bright ideas suitable for 11–18 year-olds, along with contact details and websites for voluntary organisations to get you started.

Part 1: The basics

Part 1 explains all the basics about volunteering. You'll be in good company – all kinds of celebrities do voluntary work (find out who on page 19). If you're not sure what kind of job would suit you, have a go at the quizzes. They will help you to find out what you are good at and match you to a job you will really enjoy.

Part 2: The word on the street

In Part 2 people who have done voluntary work talk about their experiences (the good and the bad!) and give you an idea of what it can be like.

Part 3: The directory

Once you have an idea of what kind of volunteering you're interested in, you're ready for Part 3 – the directory. This is the really important bit, where you can find the names and addresses of loads of different organizations. They are all listed from A–Z (starting on page 66), with a description of what they do, the voluntary work they offer, plus any age restrictions.

If you have a particular interest, such as animals, sport or people with disabilities, go to the special interest lists on page 102. If it's a particular kind of job you want, such as befriending people, outdoor work or journalism, go to the activity lists on page 108.

You can find out about jobs away from home on page 121, or if you want to volunteer for a local organization near where you live, go to page 123.

The organizations in the directory have been chosen because they make a special effort to recruit young volunteers. There are hundreds more opportunities out there but there just isn't space for them in this book! You can discover for yourself what else is on offer by doing some simple research of your own. Find out how on page 137.

Part 4: What next?

The next stage is to contact the organization you have chosen. Part 4 is full of practical information about how to go about applying, along with useful tips for interviews. Check out the advice on how to get the most out of your new volunteering job, and find out how you could help someone you know win £1,000!

IT'S A FACT

There are more than 23 million volunteers in the UK.
That's one in every three people in the street.

Every year in the UK, almost half of all people aged 16–25 do some kind of voluntary work. That means there are still about 4 million out there who haven't got round to it yet!

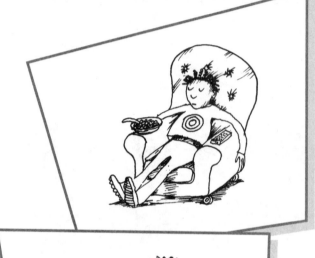

And there's a volunteering job out there to suit everyone, no matter what they want to do.

Part 1
The basics

PART 1: THE BASICS

What is a volunteer?

A volunteer is someone who:

◆ works without a profit-making motive

◆ works through free will and choice

◆ is not an employee of the organization

To put it simply, a volunteer is someone who gives their time and effort free of charge to help other people or causes.

Why do it?

If you've never volunteered before, the chances are you think it's boring, totally uncool and a waste of time. So why bother? Well, you certainly won't get rich from volunteering. On the other hand, you might discover something that you're really good at, and have a laugh at the same time.

Volunteering can give you a real head-start when you apply for a paid job. It is a no-nonsense activity which you can put on your c.v. and talk about at an interview. Lots of employers look for young people who have experience of voluntary work. It shows that you have a sense of commitment. You may also get the chance to learn new skills through volunteering, such as computer skills, which will be useful in a job.

from the horse's mouth

Name: Dianne
Job: runs a veterinary practice in Hertfordshire

"Recently I had two very capable people apply for a junior position at the surgery. I found it almost impossible to choose between them, but in the end I went for the girl who had done a significant amount of voluntary work with the local riding stables, helping disabled children to ride. I thought her experience showed she was committed and caring."

And that's just to start with. There are stacks of brilliant things to do and great people to meet. You might think that volunteers are all 'goody two-shoes' types, but really they are just ordinary people your age doing something interesting and worthwhile.

The organizations you volunteer with can give you something else that will come in handy – references. While other school-leavers may just have the standard references from their teachers, you can be one step ahead.

Some organizations offer other benefits, for example Bournemouth Helping Services in Dorset gives volunteers a Certificate of Recognition (so that you have written proof of your voluntary work). They also help you save money with a fantastic leisure card giving 10–20% discounts in shops and clubs in Bournemouth.

Many organizations pay all your expenses, such as your travel costs. When you reach age 18 or over, you may even be able to gain a qualification through volunteering. More and more voluntary organizations are joining in, for example the Cancer Research Campaign offers NVQ levels 1 and 2 (retailing) for people who volunteer in their charity shops.

You'll be surprised at the variety of voluntary work you can choose from. Anyone can be a volunteer, no matter how old you are or how little time you have to spare. Even if you only do it for an hour or a day, you're guaranteed to get something out of it. You can help people, animals or the environment and work indoors or outdoors, on your own or with a crowd. You could even join up with a group of friends to volunteer for something you are all interested in, such as a project to do with art, music, sport or computers.

from the horse's mouth

Names: Ben, Judy, Thomas, Katy, Joe
Age: 14

"I volunteer in our local hospital because it makes me feel good."

"Volunteering at the sports club gives me a sense of achievement."

"I enjoy working in our local old people's home because I don't have any grandparents."

"I volunteer in the local community as a way of making new friends with similar interests."

"I really like working with animals at the vet's surgery. I can learn about animals and enjoy myself at the same time!"

So what can volunteering give me?

New interests and hobbies ✓

A way to be part of my local community ✓

New experiences ✓

The answers to my next maths test ✗

Motivation and a sense of achievement ✓

New friends ✓

A bottomless bank account ✗

A better chance of a paid job in the future ✓

New skills ✓

Qualifications ✓

Instant attraction ☐

Celebrity volunteers: get the gossip

o you think you don't know anyone who volunteers? How about *Madonna, Ewan McGregor, Pierce Brosnan, Martin Clunes, Ross Kemp, Jude Law, Sadie Frost, Elle MacPherson, Prince Naseem, All Saints, Melinda Messenger, Robert Carlyle...?*

All of these stars helped to raise money for the NSPCC Full Stop campaign in 2000 by encouraging people to buy badges. The NSPCC's aim is to end cruelty to children once and for all. Ewan McGregor, Ross Kemp and Melinda Messenger put their faces as well as their names to the campaign, appearing on giant posters across the country to help get the message across.

Planet pop

POP STARS in particular have an impressive record for raising money for charity. The biggest landmark was the Live Aid concert back in 1985, which involved pretty much all the chart-topping acts of the day and was watched by a world-wide audience of 1.5 billion (yes, **billion**). More than £50 million was raised for famine relief in Africa – which remains the most money raised for charity by a single event.

Nice Spice

THE SPICE GIRLS have a top reputation not just for making number one singles, but also for fundraising. They donated to Comic Relief all the profits from their hit single, 'Who Do You Think You Are?' on Red Nose Day 1997. Red Nose Day has become something of a British institution thanks to the celebrities who are willing to pledge money and raise cash by doing all kinds of daft and daring things. The Spice Girls also featured on the Children's Promise Millennium album 'It's only rock and roll', along with JK of Jamiroquai, Mary J Blige, The Corrs, Fun Lovin' Criminals, Ronan Keating, Stereophonics, S Club 7… and many more. The Spice Girls' message is: "We are donating and would like to encourage all our fans to do the same."

Party in the Park

Watch the press for details of Party in the Park, a huge outdoor concert which takes place every year to raise money for The Prince's Trust (find out more about The Prince's Trust on page 92). In 2000, loads of acts performed in London's Hyde Park (in pouring rain), among them Westlife, Steps, Craig David and Travis. One hundred thousand people turned out to party all day long.

Robbie's an angel at heart

Robbie Williams, underneath his tough-guy exterior, is a nice bloke. He has set up a charitable fund, called Give it Sum, into which he put the £2 million fee that he received for being splattered in paint in a Pepsi advert. The money in the fund is going towards Robbie's chosen charities: Great Ormond Street Hospital, UNICEF, and local projects around his home town of Stoke-on-Trent. But it's not just about money. Robbie has visited Sri Lanka and Mozambique as part of UNICEF UK's 'Growing Up Alone' campaign, to draw attention to the millions of children who have been made orphans by war or AIDS. Robbie entertained crowds of children with karaoke-style renditions of 'Angels' and 'Millennium'. Afterwards he said, "Some of the best moments of my life have been those spent with children in Mozambique and Sri Lanka."

A sporting chance

Sports personalities are doing their bit, too. Tiger Woods, the number one golfer, has set up a foundation which encourages kids in deprived communities to 'dream big', as he obviously did. Tiger gives demonstrations, talks to young people and answers their questions, to help give them the confidence to be successful. Meanwhile tennis star Anna Kournikova raised the hopes of thousands of admirers when she held an online auction to raise money for breast cancer research. She put up for bid a tennis outfit that she had worn at Wimbledon, and also offered the opportunity to watch her play in a charity event in New York and hang out with her afterwards. The lucky bloke who put in the highest bid and met Anna was an 18 year-old from Indiana, USA.

Walk without fear

DAVID GINOLA takes time out from the Premier League to act as spokesperson for the 'Walk Without Fear' campaign (www.walkwithoutfear.com), which highlights the problems caused by landmines in countries such as Angola and Cambodia. David visited these countries with the Red Cross and met children who had lost limbs in landmine explosions. He wants to raise awareness of how important it is to clear all the landmines and make land safe for children to play on. David joined in a game of football with a group of kids who had artificial limbs – which gave them something to smile about for a long time to come.

Can I volunteer?

The answer is almost certainly yes. You don't have to be a pop star! And for most voluntary jobs you don't need any formal qualifications. If the job involves special skills or giving advice, the organization will make sure you have training and they will supervise anyone under the age of 18.

Usually you won't need any particular experience either, although for some jobs it's useful if you have worked with people before. If you haven't, you should receive training, help and support from the organization's volunteer co-ordinator.

Even if you think you don't have any skills to offer, bear in mind that many volunteering jobs involve just being there to talk to someone or to offer an extra pair of hands.

Voluntary organizations want to take on someone they think is suitable for the job, but they should only take relevant details into account.

A person with a criminal conviction, for example, should still be able to volunteer, although it may not be appropriate for them to do certain types of volunteering.

Exploding the myths

Number 1

You need a lot of time to be a volunteer.

Wrong!

Many organizations will welcome you even if you can only offer a small amount of time. They realize that you may not have much time to spare with school, homework, a social life and maybe a part-time job, so they offer flexible working times. You could get involved in a one-off fundraising event which only takes place once a year. Or if you decide to make a regular commitment, it might be for an hour a month or several hours a week – the choice is yours.

Number 2

Volunteering is boring and you only get the horrible jobs to do.

Wrong!

It's what you make of it. You might be asked to stick stamps on envelopes or make tea, but hang around and you're likely to be given something more interesting to do as well. And don't forget, the person in charge of you won't be psychic (well, probably not), so if you don't tell them what you want to do, they'll never know. If you want to avoid office work, then look for a volunteering opportunity that involves sport, music, art or whatever appeals to you. If you fancy something off-the-wall, try a sponsored event such as a parachute jump or sitting in a bath of cold baked beans!

Number 3

Volunteering is all about charity shops and helping old people.

Wrong!

There are volunteering opportunities to suit everyone's interests and skills. Just turn to the directory section of this book to see the huge range of different types of work. If you do your own research you can find hundreds more exciting opportunities.

How to get involved

(in a nutshell)

Hmmm...
don't know
what kind of thing
I want to do.

1. Decide what type of volunteering you want to do.
Browse through this book and have a go at the quizzes.

I'm still not sure.

2. If you can't decide or if you'd like extra advice, talk
to a friend or a teacher, or phone your local Volunteer
Bureau and make an appointment to see one of their
staff. See page 137 for contact details.

But I can't do
it every week.

3. Ask yourself how much time you can spare. For many
volunteering opportunities, you don't need to give up a
great deal of time, so choose one that suits you.

4. Think about whether you want to volunteer on your own or with friends. One of the benefits of volunteering is meeting new people, but if you don't fancy doing it on your own, get your friends involved!

5. Telephone some organizations to find out if they have any opportunities which fit the bill. Ask them to send you some information if possible.

6. Choose the one you most like the sound of and write a letter of application (see page 149). Good luck!

quiz Spotlight on you

There are loads of different reasons why people volunteer. Here are just a few ideas to get you thinking about what you want from a volunteering job. Tick the ones you agree with and fill in anything else you think of.

I want...

...to have a go at the type of work I might want to do as a full-time job. ☐

...to see a different way of life and new places. ☐

...to do more with my hobbies and interests. ☐

...to be more confident. ☐

...to do something I'm good at. ☐

quiz Match your skills

Does the thought of voicing your opinion to a roomful of people make you break out in a cold sweat? Is your worst nightmare having to wade around waist-deep in a sludgy pond? Rule number one about finding a volunteering job is to make sure it suits your personality and your interests. This quiz will help you do just that.

Fill in your answers and then read your profile, which will point you to the special interest and activity lists that might have the right organization for you. There's space at the end for you to make a note of the lists you want to look up.

		yes	no	not sure
1	I'd much rather get up and do something than sit around talking.	☐	☐	☐
2	I would like to volunteer with a group of my friends.	☐	☐	☐
3	I think I'm a good listener.	☐	☐	☐
4	My main interest is sport.	☐	☐	☐
5	I'd like to work with other people to organize fundraising and social events.	☐	☐	☐
6	I want to do something to make life better for people.	☐	☐	☐
7	I enjoy reading and writing.	☐	☐	☐

		yes	no	not sure
8	I like discussing my views and hearing what other people think.	☐	☐	☐
9	I'd like to work with animals.	☐	☐	☐
10	I'm good at making things.	☐	☐	☐
11	I enjoy using computers.	☐	☐	☐
12	I'm good at helping people to learn new things.	☐	☐	☐
13	I prefer to be on my own than in a group.	☐	☐	☐
14	I'm interested in the environment and looking after the countryside.	☐	☐	☐
15	I'd like to have my say on local issues such as improving public transport or creating play areas for children.	☐	☐	☐
16	I'd rather be outdoors than in an office.	☐	☐	☐
17	I enjoy social and group activities.	☐	☐	☐
18	I would like to set up my own community project.	☐	☐	☐

What do your answers reveal about you?

If you answered 'yes' to 1, 4, 10, 16, 18

You like to get on with things, not talk about them. Get stuck in and do something active! Outdoor or manual work could be just the thing. You might enjoy doing something for your local area, like planting trees or building sports facilities.

➡ Go to Special interest lists

Conservation, lifesaving, sport

Activity lists

Building, cooking, farming, first aid, forestry, gardening, manual work (general), outdoor work (general), painting and decorating, repairs and maintenance

---

If you answered 'yes' to 3, 6, 12

You are interested in other people and would be good at listening to someone's problems or just keeping them company. You might like to visit elderly or disabled people, or do some fundraising for charities which help people.

➡ Go to Special interest lists

Children and young people, crime concern, people with disabilities, drug education, elderly people, international aid, people with learning difficulties, poverty

Activity lists

Befriending people, caring for people, working in charity shops, dealing with problems, fundraising

If you answered 'yes' to 5, 7, 11, 13

You have skills which you could use to help with the day-to-day running of an organization. You could help out with administration, organizing events, or creating promotional material. If you like to work on your own, you may be able to do these things from home or school. Otherwise, you could gain experience of working in an office.

 Go to **Special interest lists**

Writing

Activity lists
Using computers, journalism, marketing and promotion, office work, research

If you answered 'yes' to 2, 5, 17

You are good at socializing and like to enjoy yourself! You would work well in a team. Get involved in group work, such as conservation projects, drama or music, or why not try planning social and fundraising events? The more people you can get involved, the better. If you want to make new friends, visiting and befriending people is a good way.

 Go to **Special interest lists**

Arts and crafts, conservation, drama, music

Activity lists
Befriending people, working in charity shops, outdoor work (general), teamwork (general)

If you answered 'yes' to 6, 8, 15, 18

You could talk the hind legs off a donkey! You have strong ideas and opinions, and you're good at debating. Try using your skills to help an organization campaign and gain support for their cause. You might be interested in looking into the causes of problems such as poverty and crime.

➡ Go to Special interest lists

Crime concern, drug education, environment, human rights, international aid, poverty

Activity lists

Campaigning, dealing with problems, journalism, marketing and promotion

If you answered 'yes' to 9, 13, 14

You're an animal-lover who cares about wildlife and the environment. You'd be well-suited to a practical job for a conservation charity or animal shelter. If you want to get on with a job on your own, try hands-on work with animals.

➡ Go to Special interest lists

Animals, conservation, environment

Activity lists

Farming, forestry, gardening, outdoor work (general)

Make a note

Write here the lists that you are going to look up. Then find out more about the organizations you are interested in by going to the A–Z of organizations.

> **Special interest lists** (these start on page 102)

> **Activity lists** (these start on page 108)

quiz fab or flop?

Here are some examples of volunteering jobs you could do. Which ones do you think would be worth a try? Which just don't grab you at all? Number them 1 to 15 in order of preference, considering what it is about each one that makes you switch on... or off.

a. Help on a play scheme for a week in the summer holidays, looking after children with disabilities.

b. Fundraise for a national charity by doing a one-off sponsored event with your friends. ☐

c. Serve customers in a hospital coffee bar on Saturday mornings. ☐

d. Campaign for human rights in other countries by delivering leaflets door-to-door. ☐

e. Work for an hour a week in the council offices helping to publish a community newsletter. ☐

f. Help run a youth radio station or website for a few hours a week. ☐

g. Get involved in drugs prevention by training to be a counsellor for other people your age. ☐

h. Make a video to highlight disability issues, with a group of other people your age whom you don't know. ☐

i. Now and again, offer to do some shopping for someone you know who has difficulty getting to the shops. ☐

j. Spend a weekend observing and recording local wildlife for a wildlife charity. ☐

k. Organize a youth conference on a subject such as youth crime, alcohol abuse or drug abuse. ☐

l. Read letters or books to a visually impaired person once a fortnight. ☐

m. Clean up litter from your local streets or a park with one of your mates. ☐

n. After a natural disaster, organize aid for the victims by collecting and sorting old clothes and blankets. ☐

o. Help set up a local football league for young people. ☐

Part 2
The word on
the street

PART 2: THE WORD ON THE STREET

If you're about to give volunteering a go, nothing beats hearing first-hand what it's like. Talk to friends, relatives or teachers who have done voluntary work, and see what these volunteers have to say.

funky fashions

Name: Eve
Age: 16
Volunteers with: Oxfam Originals
Job involves: working in the shop in Covent Garden, London, which sells new and second-hand designer clothes. I serve customers and sort, iron, price and display the clothes.

"It gave me a reason to get up and get out instead of vegging out at home."

"It's great fun and really cool. It's a totally different experience from school and much more interesting. I get to talk to all sorts of people I would never usually meet – people of different ages and walks of life, and tourists from all over the world. I have learnt that sometimes it's OK to make mistakes and most people are really patient and nice. It's easy to learn as a volunteer since there is no pressure, as there is when you're a paid worker.

I first started volunteering in the shop after I finished my GCSEs and had a long summer to fill up. It gave me a reason to get up and get out instead of lying in bed and vegging out at home. I spent a couple of days a week helping out in the shop until I went back to school. Unfortunately I only have time to come in one afternoon a week now I am doing my A-levels.

I enjoy making a contribution and doing something that isn't totally selfish. It's also nice being able to talk to friends at school about what I've been doing. I don't just stand about all day – recently I got to choose clothes for an Oxfam fashion shoot. Now I've got a much better idea of how much clothes are worth and what makes them worth more, which helps me when I'm buying my own clothes. Volunteering has been great fun for me."

You can get involved with charity shops by contacting any of the organizations under **Working in charity shops** (in the activity lists), or by popping into charity shops near where you live.

Pet power

Name: Jamie
Age: 13
Volunteers with: Pets As Therapy
Job involves: visiting elderly people in residential homes with my best friend, Monty. However, I usually end up taking a back seat because Monty is a ten-stone Newfoundland dog!

"I really enjoy volunteering… I feel good about helping other people."

"I really enjoy volunteering with Monty. He makes people happy by just being there and he's very gentle and docile. Well, he is now – that wasn't quite the case when he was a puppy. He looks a bit like a bear and whenever people see him they want to come over and give him a cuddle. He's just that kind of dog.

When I heard about Pets As Therapy, I knew Monty would be ideal. First he had to have an examination by the vet to make sure he was healthy. Then they gave him a biscuit and took it away again, to see how good-natured he was. He passed the test with flying colours and was awarded a badge – not that he was very impressed. He would much rather have had the biscuit.

Monty is very patient and will sit for ages letting someone stroke his head. People look so much happier and more alive just by being around him. Jenny, an elderly lady we visit, always has a few biscuits as a treat for him. When people go into a home, they often have to give their pets away. I would hate that. I have got to know the residents very well and when I had to do a school project on the Second World War, lots of them told me what it was like, as they had lived through it.

I feel good about helping other people. Scientists have done research that says stroking a cat or a dog is good for you. I can definitely agree with that. I think they should do some research on volunteering because I think they would find that is good for you too."

If you think this sounds interesting, check out the section on **Befriending people** (in the activity lists). Animal lovers can also see what's on offer in the **Animals** section (in the special interest lists). If you'd like to do what Jamie does, ring up your local residential or nursing home to see if it is part of the Pets As Therapy scheme.

Broadening horizons

Name: Andrew
Age: 17
Volunteers with: Sixty Plus
Job involves: visiting older people who have sight problems and helping them to read their post.

"When I first said I would do it I thought it might be a drag, but it's been the opposite."

"We got to know about Sixty Plus through our school. They offered us the opportunity of voluntary work as part of community service in PSHE. We didn't have to do it – only if we wanted to – but I'd been helping younger pupils with their schoolwork and enjoyed that, so I thought I would give Sixty Plus a go with my friend Susannah.

We were given training before we started, to help us imagine what it is like to be visually impaired. We had to think about how important touch, smell and sound are to people who are visually impaired, and we learnt not to insist on helping, but to let them do what they want. I think I probably took my sight for granted before the programme, but now I really appreciate it.

Susannah and I visit Pamela, who is 76, every week. I'm surprised at how much I have enjoyed it. The first time I went I wasn't sure what to talk about, but Pamela is really friendly and likes a joke. She is always interested in what we are doing and she tells us stories about family and her early life in Jamaica. I am taking a year out to go travelling and I will be in Florida while Pamela is there visiting her family, so I might take her up on her invitation to meet them. She says she tells them all about us. I think Susannah and I have both become a big part of her life.

I will probably continue with voluntary work, especially helping older people. I would like to think someone would do the same for me when I am old. Being a volunteer has helped build up my confidence and I think I have grown more mature. When I first said I would do it I thought it might be a drag, but it's been the opposite. I'm glad I offered to get involved."

Sixty Plus is based in London and contact details are on page 128. Similar opportunities are given in the special interest lists, under **People with disabilities** and **Elderly people**. You could also look in the activity lists under **Befriending people**.

Pitch in

Name: Jim
Age: 13
Volunteers with: local football club
Job involves: helping to coach younger players.

"There is a lot more to football than just playing. I hadn't really realized that before."

"I had been training in the under-14 football team myself when Neil, my coach, asked me to help out with the younger kids at summer soccer school. It was quite a big responsibility, helping the young kids develop their football skills, but I was pleased to be asked.

Before, I used to play without thinking very much about skills or tactics. But when I was coaching I had to put a lot more thought into explaining what I was doing and why I was doing it. I ended up practising a lot more so I didn't make a fool of myself when I was demonstrating what to do! Sometimes the younger kids were cheeky and difficult to handle and they didn't always listen, but other times they looked up to me and that was OK. I've got much more sympathy for the coach now. There is a lot more to football than just playing. I hadn't really realized that before.

I had never thought of being a coach, but now if I stick with it I can go on and get coaching qualifications. It is nice to see the younger kids getting better, and if one of them ends up playing for a big team I will know I helped them get there. I liked being a volunteer so I am going to do more of it. It is different from what I expected –

it's a lot more fun and I get to do things I might not get the chance to do normally. Check it out for yourself, you might find something you enjoy too!"

The best way to find out about volunteering for your local sports club is to get down there and ask what you can do to help! You can find national organizations under the heading **Sport** in the special interest lists.

Mad about animals

Name: Kelly
Age: 13
Volunteers with: Hartcliffe Community Park Farm
Job involves: looking after farm animals. Perks of the job include having a cow named after me!

"When I go for a job working with animals I can say I have plenty of experience."

"I've always loved animals but Mum put a limit on how many I could keep at home. So when I was nine I decided to help out at the community farm. That way I got to look after lots more animals than just the ones at home. There are all kinds of animals – cows, pigs, goats, sheep, ducks, rabbits, guinea-pigs and chickens. I feed them, give them attention and clean up after them.

It is hard work but I enjoy it. I've persuaded a few of my friends to come and help out as well.

I have been volunteering for four years now and I am sure I want to work with animals when I leave school. I hope that I can become an RSPCA inspector or a dog handler. When I go for a job I can say I have plenty of experience. I'll probably always come and spend time at the farm, even if it's only to visit old friends like Cuddles the rabbit. I've always been welcome here and all the people have been kind to me. It has been good fun."

Hartcliffe Community Park Farm is in Bristol, but there are similar sorts of farms all over the country. Contact the National Federation of City Farms and Community Gardens (in the A–Z of organizations) to find out more. There are other opportunities for working with animals in the special interest lists, under **Animals**.

Change your life

Name: Nigel
Age: 18
Volunteers with: The Prince's Trust
Job involves: going on a week's residential training course, then doing projects in the local community.

"I'm not sure how to sum up the experience... I just know I have turned my life around 180 degrees."

"I first found out about The Prince's Trust at the Job Centre when I was 16. I guess I was a typical teenager. I spent most of my time bored and fed up, sitting in my room playing computer games or sleeping. I had left school and I thought I knew it all. I had been in trouble with the police and ended up in prison for a while.

Then I went on The Prince's Trust residential course at Dartmoor and I realized I didn't know everything. We worked in a group learning new skills and doing challenges like getting across a river or rescuing someone who was lost. At first there were some of us who didn't get on, but eventually we became a really strong team. I did things I never thought were possible for me. And I made friendships that will last for the rest of my life, even if we don't see each other very much. It was fantastic.

After the course we had to come up with a community project. We decided to do some work on a residential home for children with disabilities, and we painted two bathrooms with a sea creatures theme. The kids loved what we did. When we saw how much it meant to them it felt really good. I saw disabled people as real people for the first time, rather than just seeing their disability.

Later I got offered a job in Kwik Fit, and a local company who sponsored us was so impressed by our team they said they would be interested in employing anyone who had completed the programme.

I'm not sure how to sum up what I got out of my time with The Prince's Trust, there was so much to it. I just know I have turned my life around 180 degrees. I discovered a lot about myself and the world that I never knew was there before. I am trying to get as many people as I can involved. It was just brilliant for me and I'm sure other people will get just as much out of it."

To get involved with The Prince's Trust, look in the A–Z of organizations for their contact details. You could also check out **Teamwork** (in the activity lists) and **People with disabilities** (in the special interest lists).

Flying high

Name: Sam
Age: 16
Volunteers with: Macmillan Nurses Fund
Job involves: fundraising by doing a sponsored parachute jump.

"The parachute jump was the most exhilarating thing I've done."

"Both my uncles died of cancer when I was younger and were cared for in their own homes by Macmillan nurses. Being able to stay in their homes instead of ending their days in hospital made a huge difference to them. I thought it would be a nice idea to raise some money in support of the Macmillan appeal. I did the usual things like shaking tins in the street, but it was boring and I wanted to raise some serious funds in a more exciting way.

When I was 15 I saw an advert in the local paper for people to raise money for Macmillan by doing sponsored parachute jumps. I thought this sounded really good fun - the only drawback was that you had to be at least 16. If I could raise £300 in sponsorship, then the cost of my jump would be reimbursed. In the end I managed to raise nearly £600, and three days after my sixteenth birthday I made my first parachute jump!

There was a group of us doing it and we spent a day being trained how to jump safely, how to use all the equipment and how to tell if things went wrong. The next day we did our jump from a small aircraft at

3,500 feet. It was the most exhilarating thing I've done. The jump was video-taped so I can relive that fantastic moment over and over again. If anyone said that raising money for charity was boring I'd say think again – the sky's the limit."

You can do fundraising in all kinds of ways for any charity you want. Contact the organization you choose and ask them to send you information on fundraising.

Sort it out

Name: Michaela
Age: 21 (16 when I started volunteering)
Volunteers with: the Quarrel Shop
Job involves: training young people in communication skills so that they can solve problems and resolve conflicts.

"It has helped me develop a lot more confidence in myself and my abilities."

"I came across the Quarrel Shop by chance when I was 16. I saw an advert at a college open day. I had never heard of it before but I had just moved to the area and it seemed like an interesting way to meet people.

I have got so much out of it. I've learned how to handle conflict in my own life more easily and I've made new friends. The Quarrel Shop trained me in communication, listening skills, problem solving and group work. You learn through drama and role-play how to deal with things like bullying, peer pressure and racial violence. All of it is creative learning rather than the kind of teaching I had at school. I used to get into a lot of trouble at school because I had learning difficulties, but the training helped me develop a lot more confidence in myself and my abilities.

When I completed my training I was asked to stay on and become a trainer helping other young participants. I have talked to groups about really sensitive issues like sex, drugs and domestic violence. All the people we train can then go on and train people themselves, so it spreads and multiplies.

One of the highlights was when I received a Young Achiever's Award from the Queen. I went to Buckingham Palace for a champagne reception with Zoe Ball. I was one of 500 people selected out of about a million people put forward. Even though volunteering meant giving up my time for free, I got a lot out of it in return. I will probably always volunteer whenever I can."

You can find contact details for the Quarrel Shop in the A–Z of organizations. If you're interested in this kind of work, look in the activity lists under **Befriending people** and **Dealing with problems**. There will also be opportunities with local groups in your area. Remember that jobs involving sensitive issues are sometimes restricted to over-18s because confidentiality is extremely important.

Disco fever

Names: Dan, Michael, Leaha and Kim
Age: 16 and 17
Volunteer with: a local youth volunteering project
Job involves: hanging out with our friends in a nightclub!
We keep an eye on under-16s on special club nights
organized for them.

"I feel like a cross between an agony aunt and a big sister."

Dan: "I started volunteering when I was 14. I didn't fancy
it to start with, but an aunt of mine persuaded me to go
along and it is a lot more fun than people make out.
Sometimes it can be annoying when people don't listen
but most of the time I enjoy it. We get loads of training
so we know how to handle most situations. We don't
get involved if there is any sort of physical trouble, but
we tend to try and sort it out before it gets that far. If
anyone does get thrown out of the club we make sure
they get a taxi home safely."

Leaha: "I feel like a cross between an agony aunt and a
big sister. The under-16s know us and they know we are
on their side, so if there are any problems they come to
us first."

Kim: "We receive training in resolving conflicts, child
protection and drug and alcohol abuse. We also learn
listening and counselling skills, which can come in useful
in our personal lives. Sometimes I remember the

conflict training and handle things better than I would have done before. Instead of getting into an argument I take a deep breath and calm down."

Michael: "Not only do you get to make new friends, you can have a dance as well!"

You may be able to do this kind of work for a youth project in your area. Look up the local organizations on page 123 for contact details.

Get afloat

Name: Ben
Age: 14
Volunteers with: Enable Holidays
Job involves: helping on a week-long canal boat holiday for young people with disabilities or learning difficulties.

"I'd recommend it to anyone!"

"The only way to sum it up is fun, exciting and rewarding! The participants are around the same age as you, so you're not there as someone bigger than them, you're just there to help with things. This means you get to know them really well. As well as going to the cinema, going swimming, helping to work the locks, cooking and playing games, you get the amazing experience of travelling by boat on the Grand Union Canal.

It feels good to help people by showing them that somebody cares whether they have a good time. I'd recommend it to anyone. You just might enjoy it as much as I did."

If you fancy going on a holiday with a difference, go to **Jobs away from home** on page 121, where you'll find details of summer camps and working holidays. There are opportunities for helping others under **People with disabilities** and **People with learning difficulties** (in the special interest lists).

Books to Africa

Name: Bouchra (Boo to my friends)
Age: 21 (14 when I started volunteering)
Volunteers with: Book Aid International
Job involves: collecting books and sending them to developing countries, particularly in Africa.

"I've always loved books, so this was a natural home for me."

"When I was 14 the librarian at my school suggested I do a story on Book Aid International for the school paper. I came to have a look round and that was it, I just kept coming back every school holiday to help out. Since I've always loved books, this was a natural home for me. Now I have a successful career here and I'm sure my volunteering experience and training helped me get the job.

I started out in the warehouse sorting and packing the books to be sent overseas. Some of the books, like children's books and textbooks, make a big difference in helping educate people. Others like the novels are just for pleasure. Either way the books are enjoyed and appreciated.

Later I was asked to help out in the office. I learnt about administration, communication, personnel and how the different departments work. I didn't realize how much I had actually gained from volunteering until I started my NVQ in Business Administration. I found I already knew most of what they were teaching me on the course!

I've made a lot of great friends whom I might never have met otherwise. In particular, two of our Book Aid International partners overseas, one in Nigeria and one in the Gambia, have become very good mates. Whenever they come over here, staff organize social evenings and on the odd occasion we tour London. We show them our country and culture and I am always welcome in their countries when I go and visit.

I think I am so lucky to work in such a great place. Part of my job now is to encourage other young people to get involved in volunteering. I know how much I got out of it, so I want others to see what is there for them if they want it."

Turn to the A–Z of organizations to find contact details for Book Aid International. For related activities, look under **Journalism** and **Research** (in the activity lists) and **Writing** (in the special interest lists).

Part 3
The directory

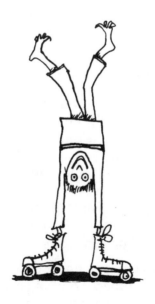

PART 3:
THE DIRECTORY

Using the directory

This directory highlights just some of the thousands of projects and activities that young volunteers are taking part in all over the UK. All of the organizations listed are on the lookout for young volunteers who want to get involved. Some of them are big charities whose names you will recognize; others are much smaller and more specialized.

A–Z of organizations

The organizations in this section take volunteers from all over the UK. Many of the organizations have branches around the country, so you can get in touch to find out about branches near where you live. Other organizations just have one office, but there will still be things you can do even if you don't live nearby. A few of the organizations arrange working holidays or summer camps. If you want to volunteer for these, it will mean working away from home.

Remember that if you can't find exactly the opportunity you're looking for in the A–Z of organizations, you can find out what else is going on in the local organizations section. There should be a wide range of opportunities available.

The directory entries are set out like this:

Friends for Young Deaf People

East Court Mansion
Council Offices
East Grinstead
West Sussex RH19 3LT
tel: 01342 323444
email: info@fyd.org.uk
website: www.fyd.org.uk

? Friends for Young Deaf People encourages volunteers to
befriend young deaf people, either by visiting them or
by writing to them.

> This is a brief description
> of what the organization does.

age 14 years

> This tells you the minimum age you
> must be if you want to volunteer for the organization.

work befriending people, fundraising, marketing and
promotion

> These are examples of the types of work you could do.
> All the terms are explained fully in the activity lists further on. You might
> find that some opportunities are not available all the time.

+ If you offer friendship to someone,
you should be prepared to visit them
or write to them regularly.

> Extra information
> which you may find useful
> is here.

Special interest lists

After the A–Z, you'll find lists which sort the organizations according to hobbies and interests they tie in with – so that you can quickly find what you're looking for. You'll find lists for everything from animals to sport to human rights. If you're interested in arts and crafts, for example, just go to the heading 'arts and crafts' to find a list of relevant organizations. Then all you have to do is look them up in the A–Z to find the contact details and more information.

Activity lists

If you want to do a particular activity or type of work, such as office work, befriending people or farming, check out the activity lists. Under each heading you'll find an explanation of what the activity involves, plus a list of organizations where you could do it. Many organizations appear in several different lists.

Jobs away from home

Do you want a volunteering job which will help you get away from it all? This section tells you what opportunities there are for working away from home, either in the UK or abroad. They range from summer camps and working holidays to year-long adventures overseas.

Local organizations

Prepare to be surprised at how many voluntary projects are going on in your local area, right under your nose, without you ever noticing! Look up the part of the country you live in to find out what organizations are working near you. Local organizations offer opportunities to suit all kinds of different interests – turn to page 123 to read some examples.

Do your own research

If you'd like to investigate volunteering opportunities for yourself, help is at hand in this section. There are loads of ideas for where to go and who to contact, including tips on how to use the Internet for research.

A-Z of organizations

1990 Trust

Southbank Technopark
90 London Road
London SE1 6LN
Tel: 020 7717 1579

? The 1990 Trust helps to voice the opinions and needs of the Black community, and encourages good relations between races.

age 14 years

work befriending people, campaigning, using computers, money matters, office work, research

Actionaid

Hamlyn House
Macdonald Road
London N19 5PG
tel: 020 7561 7565
email: admin@actionaid.org.uk
website: www.actionaid.org.uk

? Actionaid researches and tackles the causes of poverty worldwide. It helps people in extremely poor countries by educating them and improving their local facilities.

age 16 years

work using computers, fundraising, marketing and
promotion, office work

Age Concern England

Astral House
1268 London Road
London SW16 4ER
tel: 020 8765 7200
email: ace@ace.org.uk
website: www.ace.org.uk

? Age Concern promotes the well-being of older
people and helps to make life more fulfilling
and enjoyable for them.

age 16 years

work befriending people, working in charity shops,
fundraising, marketing and promotion,
office work

+ Age Concern has regional branches and charity
shops around the UK. If you want to work in charity
shops or befriend people you will need to make a
regular commitment, but it can be for any amount
of time.

Amnesty International

99 Rosebery Avenue
London EC1R 4RE
tel: 020 7814 6200
email: info@amnesty.org.uk
website: www.amnesty.org.uk

? Amnesty International works all over the world
campaigning for fair trials and the release of people who
have been unfairly imprisoned. It is also trying to bring
an end to torture and executions throughout the world.

age 16 years

work campaigning, using computers, fundraising,
journalism, marketing and promotion, money
matters, office work, research, writing newsletters

Barnardo's

Tanners Lane
Barkingside
Ilford
Essex IG6 1QG
tel: 020 8550 8822
email: david.booker@barnardos.org.uk
website: www.barnados.org.uk

? Barnardo's is the biggest and best-known children's
charity in the UK. It organizes local projects to
support children and young people in need, and their
families.

age 10 years

work arts and crafts, befriending and caring for people, building, campaigning, using computers, cooking, drama, farming, first aid, forestry, fundraising, gardening, international aid, marketing and promotion, money matters, office work, repairs and maintenance, research, sport

+ Barnardo's has regional offices around the country, providing all kinds of possibilities for young volunteers. You may be able to do teamwork or manual work, or go on a summer camp.

Bat Conservation Trust

15 Cloisters House
8 Battersea Park Road
London SW8 4BG
tel: 020 7627 2629
email: enquiries@bats.org.uk
website: www.bats.org.uk

? The Bat Conservation Trust helps look after the country's bats and their habitats. Every year it organizes a National Bat Week, when members of about 90 bat groups around the UK go out counting bats in their local area.

age 12 years

work conservation, counting and monitoring bats

Book Aid International

39–41 Coldharbour Lane
Camberwell
London SE5 9NR
tel: 020 7733 3577
email: info@bookaid.org
website: www.bookaid.org

? Book Aid International collects unwanted books to send to teachers, librarians and organizations in developing countries, particularly in Africa. It also supports local publishing projects in Africa and buys books from them.

age 12 years

work collecting and sorting books, fundraising, office work

+ Book Aid International is based in London, but anyone can get involved with fundraising and collecting books – just contact them for details.

British Deaf Association

1–3 Worship Street
London EC2A 2AB
tel: 020 7588 3520
email: info@bda.org.uk
website: www.bda.org.uk

? The British Deaf Association tries to ensure that deaf people have the same opportunities in life that other people have. It also aims to make British Sign Language more widely used and accepted.

age 16 years

work befriending deaf people, using computers, fundraising, marketing and promotion, office work

British Red Cross

9 Grosvenor Crescent
London SW1X 7EJ
tel: 020 7235 5454
email: andrea@redcross.fsnet.co.uk
website: www.redcross.org.uk

? The Red Cross works both in the UK and abroad. It provides help and first aid to people in crisis, such as people who have been injured or whose country is at war.

age 5 years

work arts and crafts, befriending and caring for other young people, learning and teaching first aid, fundraising, marketing and promotion, office work, research

+ The Red Cross runs a youth programme called Red Cross Youth, which teaches skills that you can use to help your local community. These could be first aid, rescue techniques, public speaking, leadership skills or communication skills. There are also opportunities for nursing, child care, summer camps and working outdoors.

British Trust for Conservation Volunteers (BTCV)

36 St Mary's Street
Wallingford
Oxon OX10 OEU
tel: 01491 839766
email: information@btcv.org.uk
website: www.btcv.org.uk

? BTCV is the UK's largest practical conservation charity.
Every year 85,000 volunteers take part in projects such
as planting trees, building dry stone walls and improving
footpaths.

age 16 years

work building, cooking, farming, forestry, gardening

+ Most volunteers for BTCV are involved in teamwork and
physical, outdoor activities. You may get the opportunity to
take part in a summer camp, or you could help out as a
one-off, on a spare weekend. BTCV undertakes projects
in cities as well as in the countryside. If your school or
youth group is doing conservation work, you can get in
touch with them for help and advice.

Campaign for Nuclear Disarmament (CND)

162 Holloway Road
London N7 8DQ
tel: 020 7607 3616
email: youth_cnd@hotmail.com
website: www.cnduk.org

? CND campaigns for Britain to get rid of its nuclear weapons. It has a special branch for young volunteers, called Youth and Student CND.

age 14 years

work campaigning, using computers, fundraising, journalism, marketing and promotion, office work, writing newsletters

Cancer Research Campaign

10 Cambridge Terrace
London NW1 4JL
tel: 020 7224 1333
email: volunteering@crc.org.uk
website: www.crc.org.uk

? Cancer Research Campaign investigates the causes of cancer and possible cures. It plays a major role in developing new treatments world-wide. The organization also offers support to people who have cancer.

age 16 years for working in charity shops; any age for fundraising

work working in charity shops, fundraising

+ If you work in Cancer Research Campaign charity shops, you can gain NVQ levels 1 and 2 (retailing) once you are aged 18 or over. Fundraising activities can involve anything from jumble sales to parachute jumps.

Casualties Union

PO Box 707a
Friend Street
London EC1V 7NE
tel: 020 7278 6264
email: cuhq@charity.vfree.com
website: www.casualtiesunion.org.uk

? Casualties Union recruits volunteers to act as ill or injured people so that health-care workers can practise first aid.

age 8 years

work acting as a casualty

+ As a volunteer, you have to be trained to act out the scenarios as realistically as possible. You don't have to know first aid (although it helps if you do) and you can take as long as you like to complete the training.

Cats Protection League

17 Kings Road
Horsham
West Sussex RH13 5PN
tel: 01403 221900
email: cpl@cats.org.uk
website: www.cats.org.uk

? Cats Protection League rescues stray or unwanted cats and kittens, and finds new homes for them.

age 14 years

work caring for animals, fundraising, maintaining cat shelters, marketing and promotion

Children's Express

Exmouth House
3–11 Pine Street
London EC1R OJH
tel: 020 7833 2577
email: enquiries@childrensexpress.btinternet.com
website: www.childrens-express.org

? Children's Express offers young people the opportunity to learn journalism skills and write articles for newspapers and magazines.

age 8 years

work using computers, fundraising, journalism, marketing and promotion, office work, research

+ You can do journalism for Children's Express from your own home or school, without having to go into an office. You can research and report on anything you like, from drug awareness to drama.

Community Service Volunteers (CSV)

237 Pentonville Road
London N1 9NJ
tel: 020 7278 6601
email: education@csv.org.uk
website: www.csv.org.uk

 CSV encourages young people to help others in whatever way they can, from befriending young homeless people to working with people who have learning difficulties.

age 16 years

work befriending and caring for people, building, general community work, cooking

+ CSV can find you a job to match your interests and the level of commitment you want to make. If you can spare a solid block of time, you could take on a job working away from home. You will be provided with free accommodation, food, expenses and a living allowance. CSV also links up with volunteering programmes in schools. Why not ask your school if they would like to get involved?

Crime Concern

Beaver House
147–150 Victoria Road
Swindon
Wiltshire SN1 3UY
tel: 01793 863500
email: gillian.berry@crimeconcern.org.uk
website: www.crimeconcern.org.uk

? Crime Concern aims to prevent crime, concentrating particularly on young people and how to prevent them from turning to crime.

age 14 years

work befriending people, office work, participating in action groups

+ Crime Concern runs local action groups which discuss and take action on issues such as bullying, personal safety, shop theft, drugs and vandalism.

Crusader's Union

Freepost 544
2 Romeland Hill
St Albans
Hertfordshire AL3 4BR
tel: 01727 855422
email: email@crusaders.org.uk
website: www.crusaders.org.uk

? Crusader's Union is an international youth organization which aims to reach young people with the Christian message.

age 15 years

work arts and crafts, building, cooking, fundraising, international aid, marketing and promotion, music, office work

+ As a volunteer for the Crusader's Union you can participate in youth groups, holiday camps and special events.

A-Z of organizations

Deafblind UK

100 Bridge Street
Peterborough
Cambridgeshire PE11 1DY
tel: 01733 358100
email: info@deafblind.org.uk
website: www.deafblind.org.uk

? Deafblind UK helps people who are both deaf and blind to lead full and active lives.

age 16 years

work befriending people, fundraising, marketing and promotion

Disablement Information and Advice Lines (DialUK)

St Catherine's
Tickhill Road
Doncaster
South Yorkshire DN4 8QN
tel: 01302 310123
email: dialuk@aol.com
website: members.aol.com/dialuk

? DialUK runs local advice centres across the UK. Anyone who needs information on disabilities can call in at the centre or ring them up for advice.

age 14 years

work befriending people, campaigning, using computers, fundraising, office work, research

Enable Holidays

c/o Diocesan Youth Service
Diocesan Education Centre
Hall Grove
Welwyn Garden City
Herts AL7 4PJ
tel: 01707 332321
email: stalbansdys@enterprise.net

? Enable Holidays arranges canal-boat holidays for young people who have physical disabilities.

age 14 years

work caring for young people, cooking, sport, working locks

+ The holidays take place in Hertfordshire, often during half-term school holidays. Each holiday lasts for a week and is run by volunteers.

Endeavour Children's Camps

Sheepbridge Centre
Sheepbridge Lane
Chesterfield
Derbyshire S41 9RX
tel: 01246 454957
email: john.bell@endeavour.org.uk
website: www.endeavour.org.uk

? Endeavour Children's Camps offer camping holidays for underprivileged children.

age 16 years

arts and crafts, befriending children, fundraising

Each holiday lasts for a week and they take place all over the North of England. As a volunteer, you will be working in a team with other staff, helping the children to get the most out of their holiday.

Friends for Young Deaf People

East Court Mansion
College Lane
East Grinstead
West Sussex RH19 3LT
tel: 01342 323444
email: fyd.nmtrain@charity.vfree.com
website: www.fyd.org.uk

 Friends for Young Deaf People encourages volunteers to befriend young deaf people, either by visiting them or by writing to them.

age 14 years

work befriending people, fundraising, marketing and promotion

If you offer friendship to someone, you should be prepared to visit them or write to them regularly.

Friends of the Earth

26–28 Underwood Street
London N1 7JQ
tel: 020 7490 1555
email: info@foe.co.uk
website: www.foe.co.uk

? Friends of the Earth campaigns for the protection of the environment and increases awareness about ways in which we damage our environment.

age 16 years

work campaigning, using computers, conservation, fundraising, marketing and promotion, office work

Gap Activity Projects

44 Queens Road
Reading
Berkshire RG1 4BB
tel: 0118 959 4914
email: volunteer@gap.org.uk
website: www.gap.org.uk

? Gap Activity Projects arranges voluntary projects overseas for young people who are taking time off between school and further education or employment.

age 17 years

work befriending people, building, conservation, farming, forestry, gardening, office work, teaching English as a foreign language

The projects last between six and nine months and take place all over the world, but you will have to raise money to cover your travel costs. There are loads of different projects on offer, for example, teaching English at Moscow State University; working in a YMCA camp in Ohio, USA; surveying kangaroo populations in Australia; or teaching outdoor activities such as rock-climbing and sailing in New Zealand.

Greenpeace

Canonbury Villas
London N1 2PN
tel: 020 7865 8100
email: info@uk.greenpeace.org.uk
website: www.greenpeace.org.uk

? Greenpeace aims to protect the environment by using peaceful protests and non-violent direct action.

age 16 years

work using computers, conservation, fundraising, marketing and promotion, office work, writing newsletters

The Guide Association

17–19 Buckingham Palace Road
London SW1W 0PT
tel: 020 7834 6242
email: chq@guides.org.uk
website: www.guides.org.uk

? The Guide Association is part of a world-wide organization which enables girls and young women to develop skills, make new friends and play an active part in society.

age 5 years

work arts and crafts, befriending and caring for people, childcare, cooking, conservation, first aid, sport

+ If you're female and between the ages of 5 and 26, you can get involved with the Guide Association, no matter what your race or religion. There are opportunities to do all kinds of outdoor activities, such as rafting, mountain-biking, caving, abseiling and camping.

Hand-In-Hand

c/o JLGB
3 Beechcroft Road
London E18 1LA
tel: 020 8530 8220
email: hand_in_hand@tesco.net
website: www.handinhand.8m.com

? Hand-In-Hand is a network of young Jewish people who undertake voluntary projects in their local communities.

age 14 years

work befriending elderly people, working in charity shops, fundraising, helping children with special needs, gardening, writing newsletters, designing websites

Headway - the Brain Injury Association

4 King Edward Court
King Edward Street
Nottingham NG1 1EW
tel: 0115 924 0800
email: enquiries@headway.org.uk
website: www.headway.org.uk

? Headway - the Brain Injury Association helps people to learn about head injuries. It offers information and support to people with head injuries, and their families and carers.

age 14 years

work caring for people, using computers, fundraising, office work

Help the Aged

16–18 St James Walk
London EC1R 0BE
tel: 020 7253 0253
email: info@helptheaged.org.uk
website: www.helptheaged.org.uk

? Help the Aged offers practical support to older people, to enable them to live independently.

age 16 years

work befriending elderly people, working in charity shops, using computers, cooking, gardening, marketing and promotion, office work, painting and decorating, repairs and maintenance

Hope UK

25 Copperfield Street
London SE1 OEN
tel: 020 7928 0848
email: enquiries@hopeuk.org
website: www.hopeuk.org

? Hope UK encourages children and young people to live healthy lives free from drug abuse and drink problems.

age 16 years

work fundraising, helping young people with drug or drink problems, assisting at exhibitions and other large events, public speaking

+ Volunteers speak about drug education in churches, schools and youth groups. They also take part in training sessions with parents and youth workers.

Imperial Cancer Research Fund

61 Lincoln's Inn Fields
London WC2A 3PX
tel: 020 7242 0200
Volunteering hotline: 0845 0760 700
email: j.lacey@icrf.icnet.uk
website: www.imperialcancer.org.uk

? Imperial Cancer Research Fund is concerned with the prevention, treatment and cure of all forms of cancer.

age 14 years

work campaigning, using computers, fundraising, office work

✚ Every year Imperial Cancer Research Fund holds Race for Life, a fundraising event where women all over the country do a sponsored walk or run. Girls and women of any age can take part – and if that sounds too energetic, volunteers are also needed to help organize the race!

INTERACT

Rotary International in Great Britain and Ireland (RIBI)
Kinwarton Road
Alcester
Warwickshire B49 6BP
tel: 01789 765411

? INTERACT is a network of clubs run by 11–18 year-olds. The clubs carry out volunteering projects in schools, in the local community or to benefit other countries.

age 11 years

work befriending the elderly and people with disabilities, using computers, fundraising, sport, writing newsletters

✚ The name INTERACT comes from INTERnational ACTion. Each club carries out at least two projects a year, which might involve sponsored events, organizing carnival floats, arranging speaker meetings or going on social events and days out. All INTERACT clubs are sponsored by their local Rotary Club, so you can find

out if there is a club near you by contacting your local
Rotary Club (look in your phone book or Yellow Pages).

International Voluntary Service

South England:
Old Hall
East Bergholt
Colchester
Essex CO7 6TQ
tel: 01206 298215
email: ivs@ivsgbsouth.demon.co.uk
or: ivs@ivsgbn.demon.co.uk
website: www.ivsgbn.demon.co.uk

North England:
Castlehill House
21 Otley Road
Leeds LS6 3AA
tel: 0113 230 4600

? International Voluntary Service organizes workcamps in
the UK and abroad to do a variety of voluntary projects
in local communities.

age 16 for workcamps in the UK, 18 for workcamps abroad

work arts and crafts, building, general community work,
conservation, farming, gardening, repairs and
maintainance

+ The projects are residential and last between one and
four weeks. Volunteers have to pay their own travel
costs, but accommodation and food are provided. There
is a wide variety of different types of projects available,
for example, a project in the UK might involve restoring
historic buildings, laying floors, thatching roofs and
planting vegetable gardens.

Kids' Clubs Network

Bellerive House
3 Muirfield Crescent
London E14 9SZ
tel: 020 7512 2112
email: info@kidsclubs.co.uk
website: www.kidsclubs.co.uk

? Kids' Clubs Network offers care and play facilities for primary school children, before and after school and during school holidays.

age 16 years

work arts and crafts, caring for children, cooking, drama, fundraising, marketing and promotion, sport

Macmillan Cancer Relief

89 Albert Embankment
London SE1 7UQ
tel: 020 7840 7840
email: postmasters@macmillan.org.uk
website: www.macmillan.org.uk

? Macmillan Cancer Relief aims to help people with cancer and make sure they receive the best information, treatment and care.

age 12 years

work fundraising, sponsored events, sport

National Federation of City Farms and Community Gardens

The Green House
Hereford Street
Bristol BS3 4NA
tel: 0117 923 1800
email: farmgarden@btinternet.com
website: www.farmgarden.org.uk

? This Federation supports city farms and community gardens, which are places where people join together to grow food and rear farm animals.

age 8 years

work building, caring for animals, conservation, gardening, sport

+ There are 65 city farms and 520 community gardens across the UK – find out where the nearest one to your home is. City farms are great for the environment as well as for people, as they provide a green area in built-up areas.

A-Z of organizations

National Federation of Young Farmers' Clubs

YFC Centre, National Agriculture Centre
Stoneleigh Park, Kenilworth
Warwickshire CV8 2LG
tel: 024 7685 7200
email: post@nfyfc.org.uk
website: www.nfyfc.org.uk

? The National Federation of Young Farmers' Clubs is a
group of local clubs whose members are interested in
conservation and outdoor work.

age 10 years

work conservation, fundraising, sport

+ Anyone can join their local Young Farmers' Club – you
don't need to live on a farm. You may get the chance to
take part in international exchanges, competitions and
social events.

Oxfam

274 Banbury Road
Oxford OX2 7DZ
tel: 01865 311311
email: oxfam@oxfam.org.uk
website: www.oxfam.org.uk

? Oxfam works with poor people throughout the world,
no matter what their race or religion. It aims to relieve
them from hunger, disease and poverty.

age 16 years

work working in charity shops, office work

+ If you want to work in a charity shop, you will need to make a regular commitment, even if it's only for a short amount of time. Opportunities for office work are only available at the Head Office in Oxford.

People's Dispensary for Sick Animals (PDSA)

Whitechapel Way
Priorslee
Telford
Shropshire TF2 9PQ
tel: 01952 290999
email: pr@pdsa.org.uk
website: www.pdsa.org.uk

? PDSA offers free treatment for sick and injured pets belonging to people on social security benefits.

age 14 years

work caring for animals, fundraising, marketing and promotion, office work

Prince's Trust

18 Park Square East
London NW1 4LH
tel: 020 7543 1234
freephone: 0800 842 842
email: info@princes-trust.org.uk
website: www.princes-trust.org.uk

The Prince's Trust runs courses which offer young people the chance to improve the area they live in and develop their skills and self-confidence at the same time.

age 16 years

work building, general community work, using computers, fundraising, gardening, marketing and promotion, office work, painting and decorating

As part of a Prince's Trust Volunteer team, you can join other young people from a wide range of backgrounds for a course lasting either 12 or 26 weeks. Each course starts with a week away spent getting to know each other. This year 12,000 people will gain new skills as part of a Prince's Trust Volunteer team. And there's an extra bonus for football fans – the scheme is supported by all the Premier League football clubs, and many others. They offer their grounds and facilities, and volunteers often get to meet some of the first-team players.

Project Trust

The Hebridean Centre
Isle of Coll
Argyll PA78 6TE
tel: 01879 230444
email: info@projecttrust.org.uk
website: www.projecttrust.org.uk

? Project Trust offers school-leavers the opportunity to do a year's voluntary work in a developing country.

age 17 years

work building, caring for people, general community work, office work

+ The Project Trust operates in developing countries in Latin America, Africa, the Far East and the Middle East. Activities are diverse, ranging from teaching English in Japan to working in a refugee camp in Egypt. Accommodation is basic and you will be paid local rates. You may need to fund your air fares, depending on where you go.

Quarrel Shop

Leap Confronting Conflict
8 Lennox Road
London N4 3NW
tel: 020 7272 5630
email: info@leaplinx.com
website: www.leaplinx.com

? Quarrel Shop trains young people in communication skills so that they are better able to deal with issues such as bullying, peer pressure and neighbourhood disputes.

age 16 years

work dealing with problems

+ Volunteers take part in workshops which use drama, role-play and teamwork to practise solving problems creatively.

Raleigh International

27 Parsons Green Lane
London SW6 4HZ
tel: 020 7371 8585
email: info@raleigh.org.uk
website: www.raleigh.org.uk

? Raleigh International arranges community and environmental projects overseas for young people.

age 17 years

work building, general community work, conservation, farming, sport

+ A wide range of different kinds of projects and locations is on offer, from trekking in Namibia to building bridges in Chile. You will need to raise money through sponsorship to fund your adventure.

Royal Life Saving Society UK

River House
High Street
Broom
Warwickshire B50 4HN
tel: 01789 773994
email: lifesavers@rlss.org.uk
website: www.lifesavers.org.uk

? The Royal Life Saving Society aims to reduce the number of accidents in which people drown, by training its members in lifesaving skills.

age 16 years

work training in lifesaving skills, including prevention, rescue and resuscitation

+ You will need to be able to swim if you want to volunteer for this organization.

Royal Society for the Protection of Birds (RSPB)

The Lodge
Sandy
Bedfordshire SG19 2DL
tel: 01767 680551
email: bird@rspb.demon.co.uk
website: www.rspb.org.uk

? The RSPB is concerned for birds of all kinds and protects the places in which they live.

age Any age for counting birds and nests; 16 years for other jobs

work conservation, fundraising, marketing and promotion, office work; surveying birds, bats and endangered species; working as a warden on nature reserves

+ The RSPB is Europe's largest wildlife conservation charity, with 150,000 members under 18 years old. It has a branch specially for young people, called RSPB Phoenix, which organizes projects and events. You can become a member by visiting the website.

St John Ambulance

27 St Johns Lane
London EC1M 4BU
tel: 020 7235 5231
email: youth@nhq.sja.org.uk
website: www.sja.org.uk

? St John Ambulance works world-wide saving lives and caring for sick and injured people.

age 6 years

work caring for people, communication (for example, answering telephones and directing first-aiders to where they are needed), first aid, training in lifesaving skills

✚ St John Ambulance has 57,000 volunteers, and over half of these are young people under 16. If you are aged between 10 and 16, you can join the Cadets division, which meets at least once a week to train in first aid and lifesaving skills.

A-Z of organizations

The Scout Association

Baden Powell House
65 Queens Gate
London SW7 5JS
tel: 020 7584 7030
email: baden-powell.house@scout.org.uk
website: www.scoutbase.org.uk

? The Scout Association offers young people opportunities to make friends and learn new skills by taking part in exciting adventures and challenges.

age 6 years

work arts and crafts, befriending and caring for people, cooking, conservation, first aid, sport

✚ There are different clubs for different age groups – if you're aged between 10 and 16 you can join the Scouts. If you're between 15 and 20 you can join the Venture Scouts. And it's not just for boys – girls are members too. You will get the chance to work in a team, for example doing model-making or conservation work. There are often camping trips and outings to do archery, canoeing, mountain-walking, air-weapon shooting, and much more.

Survival International

11–15 Emerald Street
London WC1N 3QL
tel: 020 7242 1441
email: info@survival-international.org.uk
website: www.survival.org.uk

? Survival International is a world-wide organization which supports tribal people and their right to live how and where they want.

age 14 years

work campaigning, using computers, marketing and promotion, office work, researching other cultures, translating

+ If you would like to translate, you will need to be fluent in a foreign language. French and Spanish are particularly useful.

Tools for Self Reliance

Netley Marsh
Southampton SO40 7GY
tel: 02380 869697
email: tools@gn.apc.org
website: www.tfsr.org

? Tools for Self Reliance collects and refurbishes second-hand tools. It sends them to Africa and Latin America to be used for building and farming.

age 14 years

work collecting unwanted hand tools and refurbishing them.

+ The organization is based in Southampton, but you can collect and repair tools in your local area, wherever you live.

A-Z of organizations

Wildlife WATCH

Wildlife Trust
The Kiln, Waterside
Mather Road
Newark NG24 1WT
tel: 01636 677711
email: info@wildlife-trusts.cix.co.uk
website: www.wildlifetrust.org.uk

? Wildlife WATCH cares for wildlife by encouraging young people to do conservation work in their local area.

age 14 years

work building, campaigning, conservation, farming, forestry, gardening, marketing and promotion, research

+ The organization has local groups around the country and also links up with schools and conservation groups. It produces action packs to tell you how you can help the environment, and it runs specific wildlife campaigns such as FrogWATCH.

Woodland Trust

Autumn Park
Dysart Road
Grantham
Lincolnshire NG31 6LL
tel: 01476 581111
email: enquiries@woodland-trust.org.uk
website: www.woodland-trust.org.uk

? The Woodland Trust owns and manages areas of woodland across the country.

age 16 years

work conservation, forestry, fundraising, gardening, public speaking about the Woodland Trust, working as a volunteer warden

+ As a volunteer for the Woodland Trust you will be doing manual work, such as clearing paths and weeds or planting trees, which you could do on a regular basis or as a one-off. If you don't live near woodland, you may need to arrange your own transport to and from woodland areas.

Woodlarks Camp Site Trust

Woodlarks Camp Site
Tilford Road, Farnham
Surrey GU10 3RN
tel: 01252 716279
email: woodlarks1@aol.com
website: www.woodlarks.org.uk

? Woodlarks Camp Site Trust offers adults and children with physical disabilities the chance to go on a camping holiday.

age 12 years

work arts and crafts, caring for people with disabilities, music, sport

+ Volunteers stay on the campsite and help to care for and entertain the campers. You would normally work for just one camp, which lasts a week, but it is possible to stay for longer. The campsite has a heated swimming pool, a trampoline and archery facilities.

A-Z of organizations

Write Away

I Thorpe Close
London W10 5XL
tel: 020 8964 4225
email: penfriends@writeaway.demon.co.uk

? Write Away arranges for children and adults with special needs and disabilities to correspond with other people by writing letters.

age 8 years

work writing letters

+ If you start a pen-friendship with someone, you should be prepared to write to them regularly.

Special interest lists

Animals

Cats Protection League
Gap Activity Projects
National Federation of City Farms and Community Gardens
People's Dispensary for Sick Animals
Royal Society for the Protection of Birds

Arts and crafts

Barnardo's
British Red Cross
Crusader's Union
Endeavour Children's Camps
The Guide Association
International Voluntary Service
Kids' Clubs Network
The Scout Association
Woodlarks Camp Site Trust

Children and young people

Barnardo's
British Red Cross
Children's Express
Community Service Volunteers
Crusader's Union
Endeavour Children's Camps
Friends for Young Deaf People
Gap Activity Projects
The Guide Association
Hope UK
International Voluntary Service

Kids' Clubs Network
National Federation of City Farms and Community Gardens
Prince's Trust
Project Trust
Raleigh International
Quarrel Shop
Write Away

Conservation

Bat Conservation Trust
British Trust for Conservation Volunteers
Friends of the Earth
Gap Activity Projects
Greenpeace
The Guide Association
National Federation of City Farms and Community Gardens
National Federation of Young Farmers' Clubs
Royal Society for the Protection of Birds
The Scout Association
Wildlife WATCH
Woodland Trust

Crime concern

Crime Concern

People with **Disabilities**

British Deaf Association
Community Service Volunteers
Deafblind UK
Disablement Information and Advice Lines
Enable Holidays
Friends for Young Deaf People
Gap Activity Projects

Headway - the Brain Injury Association
INTERACT
International Voluntary Service
One-to-One
Project Trust
Woodlarks Camp Site Trust
Write Away

Drama

Barnardo's
Kids' Clubs Network
Quarrel Shop

Drug education

Hope UK

Elderly people

Age Concern England
Community Service Volunteers
Gap Activity Projects
Hand-In-Hand
Help the Aged
INTERACT
International Voluntary Service

Environment

Friends of the Earth
Greenpeace
Survival International

Health and first aid

Casualties Union
Deafblind UK
Disablement Information and Advice Lines
Friends for Young Deaf People
Gap Activity Projects
The Guide Association
Headway - the Brain Injury Association
Hope UK
Imperial Cancer Research Fund
Project Trust
Raleigh International
The Scout Association
St John Ambulance

Human rights

Amnesty International
Survival International

International aid

British Red Cross
Crusader's Union
International Voluntary Service
National Federation of Young Farmers' Clubs
Oxfam
Project Trust
Survival International
Tools for Self Reliance

People with **Learning difficulties**

National Federation of City Farms and Community Gardens
Write Away

Special interest lists

Lifesaving

Royal Life Saving Society UK

Music

Crusader's Union
Woodlarks Camp Site Trust

Poverty

Actionaid
Barnardo's
British Red Cross
Community Service Volunteers
Endeavour Children's Camps
Oxfam
Tools for Self Reliance

Religion

Crusader's Union
Hand-in-Hand

Science

1990 Trust
Raleigh International

Sport

Barnardo's
The Guide Association
INTERACT
National Federation of City Farms and Community Gardens
National Federation of Young Farmers' Clubs
The Scout Association
Woodlarks Camp Site Trust

Writing

Amnesty International
Campaign for Nuclear Disarmament
Children's Express
Greenpeace
Hand-in-Hand
INTERACT
Write Away

Activity lists

Acting as a casualty

This means helping health-care workers to act out first-aid scenarios, with you playing the part of the ill or injured person! It's a good opportunity to find out what the organizations do and how they work.

British Red Cross
Casualties Union
St John Ambulance

Befriending people

Befriending involves visiting and supporting a person in need – it might be someone with disabilities, an elderly person or just someone who is lonely. They may need help getting around the house or they might want someone to talk to. You don't need to visit for very long each time, but you should try to visit regularly.

1990 Trust
Age Concern England
Barnardo's
British Deaf Association
British Red Cross
Community Service Volunteers
Crime Concern
Crusader's Union
Deafblind UK
Disablement Information and Advice Lines
Enable Holidays
Friends for Young Deaf People
The Guide Association
Hand-In-Hand
Help the Aged
INTERACT
International Voluntary Service
Quarrel Shop
The Scout Association

Building

Here's your chance to get stuck in and build anything from boats to birdboxes! No experience is necessary – just a bit of enthusiasm.

Barnardo's
British Trust for Conservation Volunteers
Community Service Volunteers
Crusader's Union
International Voluntary Service
Wildlife WATCH

Campaigning

As a campaigner for a charity, you'll be trying to get your message across to other people. You might be involved in writing letters to the government asking for help, or you may talk to people on the street about things that concern them.

1990 Trust
Amnesty International
Barnardo's
Campaign for Nuclear Disarmament
Disablement Information and Advice Lines
Friends of the Earth
Greenpeace
Imperial Cancer Research Fund
International Voluntary Service
Survival International
Quarrel Shop
Wildlife WATCH

Caring for people

This means looking after other people, especially doing practical things for them, such as feeding, dressing or washing. Caring can also mean just being a friend to someone and keeping them company. You should be patient and considerate to do this job.

Barnardo's
British Red Cross
Community Service Volunteers
Enable Holidays
The Guide Association
Hand-In-Hand
Headway - the Brain Injury Association

Help the Aged
International Voluntary Service
Kids' Clubs Network
National Federation of City Farms and Community Gardens
Raleigh International
The Scout Association

Working in **Charity shops**

This gives you the chance to choose, check, label and price second-hand clothes, and maybe even to let your creative talents loose on the shop displays! You'll be able to pick up some bargain buys at the same time.

Age Concern England
Help the Aged
Oxfam

Using **Computers**

If you have basic computer skills, you can help out with word-processing, desktop publishing, or creating databases and spreadsheets.

1990 Trust
Actionaid
Amnesty International
Barnardo's
Book Aid International
British Deaf Association
Campaign for Nuclear Disarmament

Activity
lists

Children's Express
Disablement Information and Advice Lines
Friends of the Earth
Greenpeace
Headway - the Brain Injury Association
Help the Aged
Imperial Cancer Research Fund
INTERACT
National Federation of City Farms and Community Gardens
Prince's Trust
Survival International

Cooking

You don't need to be a master chef to help with cooking! It involves preparing, cooking and serving food in a home, hospital, school or campsite – and anyone can join in.

Barnardo's
British Trust for Conservation Volunteers
Community Service Volunteers
Crusader's Union
Enable Holidays
The Guide Association
Kids' Clubs Network

Dealing with problems

If you're interested in social work or counselling, you can train fully once you are 18 (there is often an age restriction for this work because confidentiality is important). However, you can train now in communication skills and find out how to be a good listener. You will learn how to help other people your age who have problems, for example, with bullying or drug abuse.

Quarrel Shop

Farming

If you've never even been to a farm, you can still have a go at working on the land or with farm animals. Farming could mean general conservation, growing food, or caring for cattle, poultry, pigs and so on. You'll have to get your hands dirty (and probably the rest of your body as well).

Barnardo's
British Trust for Conservation Volunteers
National Federation of City Farms and Community Gardens
National Federation of Young Farmers' Clubs
Wildlife WATCH
Woodland Trust

Activity lists

First aid

First-aiders treat ill or injured people, and you'll need to be trained before you can do it. St John Ambulance provides really good first-aid training.

Barnardo's
British Red Cross
Enable Holidays
The Guide Association
Royal Life Saving Society UK
St John Ambulance
The Scout Association

Forestry

Forestry means looking after forests and woodland by cutting back trees, making clearings or planting new trees.

Barnardo's
British Trust for Conservation Volunteers
Wildlife WATCH
Woodland Trust

Fundraising

You can do fundraising in any way you like, for any organization you like. Let your imagination lead the way!

(On the other hand, if you're short of inspiration, call the organization and ask them to send you a fundraising information pack.)

Gardening

Have you got green fingers? Now's your chance to find out. As well as growing and caring for plants, you could help to design a garden and plant trees.

Barnardo's
British Trust for Conservation Volunteers
Hand-In-Hand
Help the Aged
International Voluntary Service
National Federation of City Farms and Community Gardens
Wildlife WATCH
Woodland Trust

Journalism

Journalism is all about getting messages and ideas over to the public. It can be in all kinds of different media, such as newsletters, radio, video or the Internet. You will need to have good writing or speaking skills and be able to communicate well.

Amnesty International
Campaign for Nuclear Disarmament
Hand-in-Hand

Manual work (general)

This involves working physically with your hands. It could be anything from digging up roads to thatching roofs.

Book Aid International
British Trust for Conservation Volunteers
Crusader's Union
International Voluntary Service
National Federation of City Farms and Community Gardens

Tools for Self Reliance
Wildlife WATCH
Woodland Trust

Marketing and promotion

Organizations have to market and promote themselves
forcefully so that they receive enough money and voluntary
support. You can help to organize advertising campaigns, run
special events or design posters and leaflets.

Actionaid
Age Concern England
Amnesty International
Barnardo's
Book Aid International
British Deaf Association
British Red Cross
Campaign for Nuclear Disarmament
Cats Protection League
Children's Express
Crusader's Union
Deafblind UK
Friends for Young Deaf People
Friends of the Earth
Greenpeace
Hand-In-Hand
Help the Aged
Imperial Cancer Research Fund
Kids' Clubs Network
People's Dispensary for Sick Animals
Prince's Trust
Quarrel Shop
Royal Society for the Protection of Birds
Survival International
Wildlife WATCH

Money matters

Money matters involves office work related to an organization's finances, such as recording donations. You will need to use basic maths skills.

1990 Trust
Amnesty International
Barnardo's

Office work

If you volunteer to work in an office, you may be able to try your hand at all kinds of different tasks, such as word-processing, filing, sending out letters and leaflets, updating records and databases, or ringing up people for information. You will need to use basic maths and English skills and you'll be dealing with a wide range of people.

1990 Trust
Actionaid
Age Concern England
Amnesty International
Barnardo's
Book Aid International
British Deaf Association
British Red Cross
Campaign for Nuclear Disarmament
Children's Express
Community Service Volunteers
Crime Concern
Crusader's Union
Disablement Information and Advice Lines
Friends of the Earth
Greenpeace

Activity lists

Headway -the Brain Injury Association
Help the Aged
Imperial Cancer Research Fund
International Voluntary Service
National Federation of City Farms and Community Gardens
People's Dispensary for Sick Animals
Prince's Trust
Quarrel Shop
Raleigh International
Survival International

Outdoor work (general)

This covers any activity at all that you do outside instead of in a building – so if you hate sitting at a desk, this is for you! There are as many opportunities for working outdoors in a city as there are in the countryside.

Barnardo's
British Red Cross
British Trust for Conservation Volunteers
Crusader's Union
Endeavour Children's Camps
The Guide Association
Help the Aged
International Voluntary Service
National Federation of City Farms and Community Gardens
National Federation of Young Farmers' Clubs
Raleigh International
The Scout Association

Painting and decorating

Have a go at painting and decorating and find out how much fun it can be. Volunteers are always needed to decorate hospitals, community centres, old people's homes and youth clubs.

Barnardo's
Hand-In-Hand
Help the Aged

Repairs and maintenance

Repairs and maintenance is for anyone who likes working with their hands, making or repairing things. Enthusiasm and a willingness to learn are more important than experience.

Barnardo's
Cats Protection League
Hand-In-Hand
National Federation of City Farms and Community Gardens
Raleigh International

Research

Research means collecting information, for example, by using libraries or the Internet, or by talking to people. The information may then be used in books, reports or brochures produced by the organization. You could also choose to work in libraries or resource centres run by voluntary organizations.

1990 Trust
Amnesty International
Barnardo's
British Red Cross
Children's Express
Disablement Information and Advice Lines

Activity lists

Royal Society for the Protection of Birds
Survival International
Wildlife WATCH

Teamwork (general)

Teamwork encourages you to work well with other young people, which means listening to each other's opinions and deciding together on the best way to do something. It will give you skills in leadership and dealing with other people.

Barnardo's
British Trust for Conservation Volunteers
Children's Express
Community Service Volunteers
Crime Concern
Crusader's Union
Endeavour Training Ltd
The Guide Association
International Voluntary Service
Prince's Trust
Raleigh International
The Scout Association
Wildlife WATCH
Woodland Trust

Translating

Organizations sometimes need to translate written material from other countries. You can do this if you are fluent in a foreign language – French and Spanish are particularly useful.

Survival International

Jobs away from home

If you want to spice up your school holidays, think about volunteering for an organization which runs summer camps, for example for children with disabilities, or for children who don't normally have the chance to go on holiday. Volunteers are needed to help out with jobs such as cooking, organizing activities and making sure the participants are all safe and enjoying themselves. It gives you the chance to get away from home, meet new people and do something completely different.

Find out more by contacting one of these organizations, all of which run summer camps:

Barnardo's
British Red Cross
British Trust for Conservation Volunteers
Crusader's Union
Endeavour Children's Camps
Hand-In-Hand
Kids' Clubs Network
National Federation of City Farms and Community Gardens
Woodlarks Camp Site Trust

There are opportunities to do other kinds of work away from home, which might involve just about any kind of voluntary work you can think of! You could get a job doing conservation work, befriending young homeless people or restoring old monuments. It might be just for a few days, or could be for up to a year or more.

Voluntary jobs in other countries offer the prospect of an exciting adventure. The not-so-good news is that opportunities are fairly limited for people under 21, and you will usually have to pay your travel costs, which might be as much as £2,000. So unless you've won the lottery, you will need to spend a lot of time fundraising and asking for sponsorship before you go.

These organizations have opportunities for working away from home, either in the UK or abroad:

Community Service Volunteers
Enable Holidays
Gap Activity Projects
International Voluntary Service
Project Trust
Raleigh International

If you would like more advice and information about working as a volunteer overseas, try contacting:

Returned Volunteer Action
1 Amwell Street
London EC1R 1UL
tel: 020 7278 0804

Local organizations

There are local organizations all over the UK which do all kinds of projects that benefit the local community. This section features many of the organizations which are based in large towns and cities. The organizations are divided up into areas of the country – Southeast England, Southwest England, Wales, Midlands and East Anglia, Northeast England, Northwest England, Scotland, and Northern Ireland. Simply look up the part of the country you live in and flick through to find the nearest one to where you live.

A few of these organizations specialize in a certain activity, such as music or conservation. These are marked with a star, like this: ★. You can read about exactly what the organization does and what opportunities are offered. The rest of the organizations are general ones which have a range of volunteering opportunities. They will be able to tell you what organizations are currently working in your area, and how to link up with them.

To give you an idea of the sort of volunteering jobs which might be on offer at any of these local organizations, here are some examples from Bournemouth Helping Services in Dorset:

● Organizing and supervising activities for other young people at Dorset Christian Activity Centre. Activities include rock-climbing, quad-biking and canoeing – and you have the opportunity to become a qualified instructor.

● Volunteering with Help and Care, a charity which supports older people and carers. Jobs include fundraising, helping with mailings and exhibitions, conducting safety checks at the homes of older people, and working with professional health visitors.

Local organizations

- Helping to support people with mental health problems in adult education classes.

- Working on film and media projects in which young people share their views with the local community.

- Working in Oxfam shops – choosing, buying and pricing stock, serving customers and helping with marketing campaigns.

- Supporting and befriending young pregnant girls with Platform for Young Women.

- Helping with Books on Wheels, a mobile library organized by the Women's Royal Voluntary Service.

- Helping in the Bournemouth Hospital Coffee Shop.

- Producing posters and a video documentary for the Boscombe Network for Change – a young people's group which fights drug abuse, homelessness and poverty.

- Helping people with disabilities to go sailing at Rockley Sailing School.

- Doing ground maintenance at Bournemouth Football Club.

- Working on the committee of Bournemouth Youth Council, representing young people's views on youth groups, leisure facilities and jobs.

- D-Jing for Bournemouth Youth Service at local youth club discos.

- Clearing disused railway tracks to make walkways, with the British Trust for Conservation Volunteers.

- Painting a mural and making banners for International Women's Day – a day which celebrates womanhood, motherhood and the role of women all over the world.

Southeast England

Bedfordshire

Bedfordshire Royal Community Charity
The Old School
Cardington
Bedford MK44 3SX
tel: 01234 838771

Youth Action Bedford
Bedford Centre for Voluntary Service
43 Bromham Road
Bedford MK40 2AA
tel: 01234 350458

Berkshire

Reading Youth Action
Reading Activity Centre
69 Bulmershe Road
Reading RG1 5RP
tel: 0118 901 5636

Wokingham District Volunteer Development Agency
9 Headley Road
Woodley
Reading RG5 4JB
tel: 0118 969 1551
freephone volunteer line:
0800 056 3940
email: info@wdvda.org.uk
website: www.wdvda.org.uk

Buckinghamshire

Aylesbury Youth Action
Queen's Park Centre
Queen's Park
Aylesbury HP21 7RT
tel: 01296 421149

Wycombe Youth Action
The Round House
St Mary's Street
High Wycombe
HP11 2HE
tel: 01494 447250

Local organizations

Cambridgeshire

Cambridgeshire Association of Youth Clubs
Paston Ridings Farm
Paston Ridings
Peterborough PE4 7XB
tel: 01733 574455

Youth Action Cambridge
Shaftesbury House
22 Godestone Road
Cambridge CB5 8HR
tel: 01223 316105

East Sussex

Make a Difference Project
Hastings Trust
35 Robertson Street
Hastings TN34 1HT
tel: 01424 446373

Police Community Safety Unit
Police Station
Terminus Road
Bexhill-on-Sea TN39 3NR
tel: 01424 456153

Essex

Havering Youth Volunteering Project
Robert Beard Youth Centre
233 High Street
Hornchurch RM11 3XU
tel: 01708 474290

Hampshire

Eastleigh Youth Volunteering Project
Eastleigh Community Services
16 Romsey Road
Eastleigh SO50 9AL
tel: 023 8090 2400

Hampshire County Council County Youth Service
Horndean Youth Club
Horndean Community School
Barton Cross
Portsmouth PO8 9PQ
tel: 023 9259 9371

Hertfordshire

Stevenage Youth Volunteers
Stevenage Youth Volunteer Bureau
Bowes Lyon House
6 Georges Way
Stevenage SG1 1XY
tel: 01438 747171

Kent

Sevenoaks VSU Youth in Action
The Bradbourne School
Bradbourne Vale Road
Sevenoaks TN13 3LE
tel: 01732 450448

Tunbridge Wells VSU Youth in Action
The Jukebox
c/o Tunbridge Wells Girls' Grammar School
Southfield Road
Tunbridge Wells TN4 9UJ
tel: 01892 531584

London

Action Southwark
727 Old Kent Road
London SE15 1NY
tel: 020 7358 0690

Army Cadet Force
E Block
Duke of York's Headquarters
London SW3 4RR
tel: 020 7730 9733
website:
www.armycadets.com

Army Cadet Force organizes teams of young people aged 13 and over to do outdoor challenges, such as field training and expeditions. It offers citizenship training and the chance to develop yourself both physically and mentally.

Islington Volunteer Centre
65–69 White Lion Street
London N1 9PP
tel: 020 7833 9690

Faces in Focus
102 Harper Road
London SE1 6AQ
tel: 020 7403 2444

Local organizations

Paddington Arts
32 Woodfield Road
London W9 2BE
tel: 020 7286 2722

Paddington Arts is a youth arts and media organization which offers workshops in dance, drama and singing for anyone aged six and over. It also provides opportunities to make videos and take part in community festivals.

The organization owns a farm in Somerset where young people can go for a week to experience life in the country, looking after animals and picking vegetables.

 Sixty Plus
1 Thorpe Close
London W10 5XL
tel: 020 8969 9105
email: SixtyPlus@hotmail.com

Sixty Plus supports older people living in Kensington and Chelsea and helps them to continue living independently. It arranges for young people aged 16 and over to visit older people to befriend and help them.

Volunteer Action Tower Hamlets
179–181 Whitechapel Road
Davenant Centre
London E1 1DW
tel: 020 7377 0956

Youth Action Volunteering
Albany Youth and Community Centre
Bell Lane
Enfield EN3 5PA
tel: 020 8443 3586

Surrey

Reigate and Redhill YMCA
Prince's Road
Redhill
Surrey RH1 6JJ
tel: 01737 779979

West Sussex

Outset Youth Action County Office
Lodge Hill Centre
Watersfield
Pulborough RH20 1LZ
tel: 01798 831153

Southwest England

Bristol

Young Bristol
113 Parson Street
Bedminster
Bristol BS3 5QH
tel: 0117 953 7921
website:
www.youngbristol.demon.co.uk

Cornwall

North Cornwall Youth Volunteer Network
Community Projects Trust
(S.W.) Ltd
2a Fore Street
Mount Folly
Bodmin
Cornwall PL31 2HQ
tel: 01579 342438

Devon

BTCV
171 Sidwell Street
Exeter EX4 6RH
tel: 01392 666463

Exeter Volunteer Bureau
c/o Exeter CVS
Wat Tyler House
King William Street
Exeter EX4 6PD
tel: 01392 202055

Help at Hand
149 High Street
Ilfracombe EX34 9EZ
tel: 01271 866555

Dorset

Bournemouth Millennium Volunteers
Bournemouth CVS
3–5 Palmerston Road
Boscombe
Bournemouth BH1 4HN
tel: 01202 467000
email: bmthhelpingservices@cwcom.net

Gloucestershire

Glosaid Youth Action
Chequers Bridge Youth Centre
Painswick Road
Gloucester GL4 9PR
tel: 01452 304227

Local organizations

Herefordshire

One to One
Community Council of
Hereford and Worcester
41a Bridge Street
Hereford HR4 9DG
tel: 01432 267820

Isle of Wight

Island Volunteers
39 Quay Street
Newport PO30 5BA
tel: 01983 527333

Somerset

**Yeovil Youth Volunteering
Project**
Room 4, 19–20 High Street
Yeovil BA20 1RX
tel: 01935 414023

Worcester

Millennium Volunteers
Worcester City Volunteer
Bureau
33 The Tything
Worcester WR1 1JL
tel: 01905 24741

Wales

 **Community Music
Wales**
2 Leckwith Place
Canton
Cardiff CF11 6QA
tel: 029 2038 7620
email: projects@community
musicwales.org.uk
website: www.community
musicwales.org.uk

Community Music Wales
provides access to musical
instruments and equipment
for schools, hospitals, youth
groups and people with
learning difficulties.

People aged 14 and over do
workshops and performances
across Wales and you can get
involved no matter how
much or little musical
experience you have.

Youth Link
91a Cardiff Road
Caerphilly
South Wales CF83 1FQ
tel: 029 2088 5711

Midlands and East Anglia

Birmingham

Birmingham Volunteer Action
Birmingham VSC
138 Digbeth
Birmingham B5 6DR
tel: 0121 643 4343

Birmingham Youth Volunteers Project
4th Floor
Smithfield House
Digbeth
Birmingham B5 6BS
tel: 0121 622 2888

 ### Groundwork Foundation
85–87 Cornwall Street
Birmingham B3 3BY
tel: 0121 236 8565
email:
info@groundwork.org.uk
website:
www.groundwork.org.uk

Groundwork Foundation works in partnership with local businesses and the government to improve the environment and facilities in the local area. If you are 16 or over, you can get involved with marketing and promotion, office work or carrying out surveys on the environment.

Derbyshire

Young People... Make a Difference
Derby YMCA
London Road
Wilmorton
Derby DE24 8UT
tel: 01332 751707

Leicestershire

Leicestershire CVYS
2 Tower Street
Leicester LE1 6WR
tel: 0116 254 3724
email: cvys.llr@virgin.net

Loughborough Volunteer Centre
John Storer House
Wards End
Loughborough LE11 3HA
tel: 01509 224900

Local organizations

Norfolk

Norwich and Norfolk Voluntary Services
Charing Cross Centre
17–19 St John Maddermarket
Norwich NR2 1DN
tel: 01603 614474

Nottinghamshire

Nottingham Millennium Volunteers
City of Nottingham Central Library
3 Angel Row
Nottingham NG1 6HP
tel: 0115 915 3754

Rushcliffe Youth Action Network
Park Lodge
Bridgford Road
West Bridgford NG2 6AT
tel: 0115 981 6988

Sutton Volunteer Bureau
The Old Police Station
Brook Street
Sutton-in-Ashfield
Nottingham NG17 1AL
tel: 01623 515614

Northeast England

Hartlepool

Hartlepool Voluntary Development Agency
'Rockhaven'
36 Victoria Road
Hartlepool TS26 8DD
tel: 01429 262641

Hull

Youth Action Hull
Mitchell House
78 Spring Bank
Hull HU3 1AB
tel: 01482 328965

South Yorkshire

Rotherham Make a Difference Volunteer Project
The Guardian Centre
Drummond Street
Rotherham S65 1HY
tel: 01709 366654

Young Volunteers Agency
Voluntary Action Barnsley
35 Queen's Road
Barnsley S71 1AN
tel: 01226 242726

Tyne & Wear

Gateshead Borough Youth Organizations Council
6 Regent Terrace
Gateshead NE8 1LU
tel: 0191 490 1900

North Tyneside VODA
The Linskill Centre
Linskill Terrace
North Shields NE30 2AY
tel: 0191 200 5790

South Tyneside Youth Action Volunteers
Stanhope Complex
Gresford Street
South Shields NE33 4SZ
tel: 0191 454 8704

Voluntary Services Dept.
Gd. Floor
Milvain Building
Newcastle General Hospital

Westgate Road
Newcastle upon Tyne
NE4 6BE
tel: 0191 256 3203
email:
christine.lopez@northy.nhs.uk

Youth Information Shop
Gateshead Metro Centre
45 Garden Walk
Gateshead NE11 9XZ
tel: 0191 461 1999
email: info@yinet.org.uk
website: www.yinet.org.uk

West Yorkshire

Batley Youth Action
The Young Batley Centre
Thomas Street
Cross Bank
Batley WF17 8PR
tel: 01924 326235

Bradford Youth Volunteering Development Project
Bradford CVS
19–25 Sunbridge Road
Bradford BD1 2AY
tel: 01274 722772

Local organizations

Hebden Bridge Youth Action
Unit 1, 38 Hangingroyd Lane
Hebden Bridge HX7 7DD
tel: 01422 842308

MV Project
c/o Shipley and Baildon
Volunteer Bureau
14 Commercial Street
Shipley
West Yorkshire BD18 3SP
tel: 01274 599441
email@mv@care4free.net

Youth Volunteer Development Project
Voluntary Action – Wakefield
District
11 Upper York Street
Wakefield WF1 3LQ
tel: 01924 367418

Northwest England

Bolton

Bypass
106–108 Newport Street
Bolton BL3 6AB
tel: 01204 362002

Peer Mediation Project
The Base
Marsden Road
Bolton BL1 2PF

Cheshire

Congleton and District Youth in Action
c/o Flat 6, Meadow Hill
Court
Park Road
Congleton CW12 1DA
tel: 01260 275467

Cumbria

County Youth Service
John Winnerah Institute
Abbey Road
Barrow-in-Furness
LA14 1XN
tel: 01229 894433

Liverpool

John Moores University Students Union

The Haigh Building
Maryland Street
Liverpool L1 9DE
tel: 0151 231 3583

Manchester

Millennium Volunteers
Tameside Young People's
Centre
Duke Street
Denton
Manchester M34 2AN
tel: 0161 336 6615

Youth Info Shop
1 Market Arcade
Northwich
South Manchester
tel: 01606 353520
e-mail: youthinfoshop@
rcvs.demon.co.uk

Youth Information Shop
14 King Street
Bacup
North Manchester
OL13 0AH
tel: 01706 879194

Salford

Salford Volunteer Bureau

12 Irwell Place
Eccles
Salford M30 0FN
tel: 0161 707 7067

Wirral

Wirral Action
Elm House
Elm Street
Birkenhead CH41 4AR
tel: 0151 647 8198

Local organizations

Scotland

Breakthrough Youth Project
304 Maryhill Road
Glasgow
G20 7YE
tel: 0141 331 0110

North Glasgow Community Forum
Ardoch House
25 Ardoch Street
Glasgow G22 5QG
tel: 0141 564 1030

Replies Youth Information Project
c/o Hillhead CE Centre
169 Meiklehill Road
Kirkintilloch
Glasgow G66 2JT
tel: 0141 777 7791

Youth Enquiry Service
170 High Street
Cowdenbeath
Edinburgh KY4 9NH
tel: 01383 510101
email: yes-yes@nfyes.co.uk

Northern Ireland

Challenge for Youth
40–46 Edward Street
Belfast
BT17 OPP
tel: 028 9023 6893

Strabane District Initiative for Youth
17 Dock Street
Strabane
BT82 8EE
tel: 028 7188 5498

Youth Action Northern Ireland
O'Fiaich House
25 Cardinal O'Fiaich Square
Crossmaglen
Newry
County Down
BT35 9HG
tel: 028 3086 8734

Doing your own research

You can see that there are loads of volunteering opportunities in this book, but it can be really rewarding to do your own research and find out for yourself what else is out there. And it's a piece of cake too – with libraries, volunteering associations and websites all ready and waiting to point you in the right direction. Here are some tips...

● Look in your phone book under 'Volunteer Bureaux', or contact this address for details of your nearest one:

National Association of Volunteer Bureaux
New Oxford House
16 Waterloo Street
Birmingham B2 5UG
tel: 0121 633 4555
email: info@navb.co.uk
website: www.navb.org.uk

● Browse through your local newspaper – you'll probably come across news features or adverts about projects that young people are involved in. You could also try looking in your Yellow Pages under:

Charitable organizations   Information services
Clubs and associations   Social service and welfare
Conservation organizations   Sports clubs and associations

● There may be an organization in your area set up specifically to support and encourage young volunteers. These organizations are known as 'Youth Action Agencies'. They offer young people a wide range of opportunities and aim to make sure they get the most out of their volunteering. Try looking in your Yellow Pages under 'Youth action agencies' or 'Youth and community groups'.

● Pop into your local library and you will find information on local organizations catering for a wide range of interests. Tell the librarian what sort of volunteering job you are after, and he or she will help you to search the resources.

● Also in your local library, have a look at the 'Voluntary Agencies Directory', which you will find in the reference section. This is a totally comprehensive list of all the national voluntary organizations in the UK. There are about 2,500 in total, so you won't be stuck for more ideas and people to contact!

● Many young people become involved in volunteering through the Youth Service, which is run by your local council. It sets up and runs youth clubs in your area to encourage young people to take action in their community. You can get details of local youth groups and projects by looking in your Yellow Pages under 'Youth and Community Groups' or by ringing the Youth Service in your area. This is usually based in the education department of your local authority.

● Buy the Guardian newspaper on a Wednesday. It lists new volunteering opportunities every week in the jobs section. These won't necessarily be aimed at young people, so when you contact an organization, ask whether their opportunities are open to people your age.

● Find out about some of the work done by charities and community groups by tuning in to the Community Channel (channel number 655). This is a non-subscription service on Sky TV. It will give you more ideas of how to get involved in volunteering.

Youth for Britain

Youth for Britain is an organization which has loads of information about volunteering opportunities in the UK and world-wide. There are several ways you can use their services.

● Search the computerised database 'Youth for Britain'. You will find this database in most libraries, schools, career offices and volunteer bureaux. It is simple to use, with on-screen instructions and categories to tick, and it should come up with a number of opportunities to suit you.

● Check out the book *Worldwide Volunteering for Young People*, which is a printed directory of the information on the database. It is published by How To Books and priced £15.95. You can buy it from bookshops or direct from Plymbridge Distributors Ltd tel: 01752 202301.

● Get in touch with Youth for Britain and ask them to carry out a search of volunteering opportunities for you. They will make a small charge for this service. Contact:

Youth for Britain
Higher Orchard
Sandford Orcas
Sherborne
Dorset DT9 4RP
tel: 01963 220773

● Youth for Britain's listings contain details of national organizations which welcome young volunteers. They can tell you if there is a branch of any particular organization in your area. Remember to enclose a stamped addressed envelope if you write to them.

Using the Internet

Explore the Internet for up-to-the-minute information about what's on offer. Try using a search engine such as HotBot, Altavista, Infoseek, Excite or Lycos.

If you want to find general information on volunteering on the web, try the following sites.

www.nya.org.uk
This is the website of the National Youth Agency, which supports young volunteers. Here you will find information on:
● becoming a volunteer
● volunteering opportunities
● voluntary organizations
● overseas voluntary work
● volunteering in conservation

www.youthnet.org.uk/do-it
or **www.thesite.org/do-it**
Youth Net UK has a section of its website dedicated to
volunteering. They have lists of volunteering opportunities
which you can look through to find those nearest to your
home, or you can chat with other volunteers in the UK and
world-wide and post your own personal message about your
volunteering experience on the site's noticeboard. There is
also a mine of information about volunteering and an agony
aunt service for anyone needing advice.

www.volunteering.org.uk
This is the site of the National Centre for Volunteering. It can
help answer your questions about volunteering and has all the
latest facts and figures. The Centre itself does not organize
volunteering jobs, but the website has links to other sites
which can put you in touch with voluntary groups.

www.millenniumvolunteers.gov.uk
Millennium Volunteers is a UK-wide initiative for 16–24 year-
olds who want to volunteer their time for the benefit of
others. It is funded by the government and there are 160
projects running around the country. The organisation does
not arrange voluntary work, but they can put you in touch
with local organisations.
Their head office address is:
MV Unit
Room N2
DfEE
Moorfoot
SHEFFIELD S1 4PQ
tel: (Freephone) 0800 917 8185
email: millennium.volunteers@dfee.gov.uk

Doing your
own research

www.bbc.co.uk/education/timebank
Check out the BBC's TimeBank scheme. All you have to do is
send them your details and the amount of time you want to
give, and you'll receive a list of organizations in your area to
match your interests.

The Changemakers scheme

Volunteering doesn't have to mean striking out on your own
and joining an organization. You can do voluntary work in
your own school, with the help of the Changemakers
scheme. Changemakers run a variety of activities in schools
all over the UK, to get pupils interested in volunteering.
Why not find out if your school would like to get involved?
You can contact Changemakers at:

Changemakers
Baybrook Farm
Lower Godney
Nr Wells
Somerset BA5 1R2
tel: 01 4588 834767

Here are some of the things that Changemakers are
helping pupils to do in schools around the country:

● improve an area of wasteland near the school.

● give drama presentations at local primary schools on the
theme of going to secondary school.

● organize a five-a-side football club to raise money for local
charities.

● construct a BMX facility for local young people to use.

● stage a disco to raise money for the heart unit at a local hospital.

● look at the effects of business on the environment and present their findings to local business people.

● make a tape of stories for partially sighted children.

Religious organizations

Lots of voluntary work is done by religious groups, who often have youth networks to help young people get involved in volunteering activities. Contact any of these organizations to find out more.

Board of Deputies of British Jews
Commonwealth House
1–19 New Oxford Street
London WC1A 1NU
tel: 020 7543 5400

Buddhist Society
58 Eccleston Square
London SW1V 1PH
tel: 020 7834 5858

Churches Together in Britain and Ireland (CTBI)
35–41 Lower Marsh
London SE1 7RL
tel: 020 7620 4444

Interfaith Network
5–7 Tavistock Place
London WC1H 9SN
tel: 020 7388 0008

Islamic Cultural Centre
146 Park Road
London NW8 7DG
tel: 020 7724 3363

National Council of Hindu Temples
40 Stoke Row
Coventry CV2 4JP
tel: 0121 622 6946

Sikh Council for Inter-faith Relations
43 Dorset Road
Merton Park
London SW19 3EZ
tel: 020 754 4148

Part 4
What next?

PART 4: WHAT NEXT?

Narrow it down

By now you'll probably have some ideas about which voluntary organizations you are interested in, and hopefully there will be several organizations that you would like to contact. List them here and make a note of what you find out when you contact them.

Name of organization: _____

Name of volunteer co-ordinator: _____

Details of opportunities: _____

_____

_____

_____

Name of organization: _____

Name of volunteer co-ordinator: _____

Details of opportunities: _____

_____

_____

_____

Name of organization: _____

Name of volunteer co-ordinator: _____

Details of opportunities: _____

_____

_____

_____

Name of organization: _____

Name of volunteer co-ordinator: _____

Details of opportunities: _____

_____

_____

_____

Name of organization: _____

Name of volunteer co-ordinator: _____

Details of opportunities: _____

_____

_____

_____

How to apply

The next step is to get your volunteering job lined up. Here's what to do...

1
The decision
Make a shortlist of organizations (see pages 146–147), then decide which is your number one choice and try this first.

2
The phone call
Phone the organization and ask to speak to the volunteer co-ordinator. Find out from him or her what opportunities are available. Or you can write a letter saying what you're interested in doing and asking about suitable opportunities.

3
The letter
Write to the volunteer co-ordinator confirming that you are interested in volunteering for them (have a look at the letter-writing hints on the opposite page).

4
The interview
If you are asked to visit the organization for an interview, check out the tips on page 154 before you go.

5
Find out more
When you visit, ask the volunteer co-ordinator everything you need to know, such as what training and supervision you will receive. Don't be afraid to ring up afterwards to ask more questions.

6
Is the job right for you?
Make sure that both you and the volunteer co-ordinator understand how much time you are going to put in. If you're not sure whether you want to take on the job, go home and think about it (but remember to let them know your decision as soon as you can).

Letter-writing hints

When you write to an organization, make sure your letter is clear and to the point. Don't write an essay! One side of A4 is plenty. Either word-process it on a computer or hand-write it neatly.

It might look something like this:

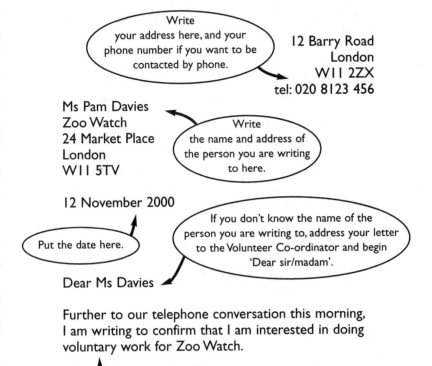

Write your address here, and your phone number if you want to be contacted by phone.

12 Barry Road
London
WII 2ZX
tel: 020 8123 456

Ms Pam Davies
Zoo Watch
24 Market Place
London
WII 5TV

Write the name and address of the person you are writing to here.

12 November 2000

Put the date here.

If you don't know the name of the person you are writing to, address your letter to the Volunteer Co-ordinator and begin 'Dear sir/madam'.

Dear Ms Davies

Further to our telephone conversation this morning, I am writing to confirm that I am interested in doing voluntary work for Zoo Watch.

Start by saying why you are writing. If you have already made contact with the person or organization, say so at the outset.

Say a bit about yourself and why you would like to volunteer. Tell them what jobs in particular you want to do.

I am 14 years old and I would like to study veterinary science when I leave school. At home we have two dogs and a hamster, but I would like to gain some experience of working with larger animals at Zoo Watch. I am hardworking and reliable and am willing to do cleaning, animal food preparation and any other duties that may be necessary. However, I particularly want to work directly with the animals. I live locally, so transport would not be a problem.

My interests are drama, biology and sport, and I play on the school under-15s netball team.

Mention your hobbies and interests.

I have already done some voluntary work for the RSPCA, which involved walking dogs and cleaning kennels. I enjoyed this and I am now looking for something a bit more challenging.

If you have already done some volunteering, say what sort of work you did and who it was for.

I enclose a stamped addressed envelope for your reply and look forward to hearing from you soon.

Yours sincerely

Kirsty Hall

Kirsty Hall

End with 'Yours sincerely' and your signature. Print your name clearly underneath.

How to begin a letter

If you're stuck for words to begin your letter, use one of these openers:

1   I have heard about the voluntary work being carried out by [name of organization] and I would like to know if I can help in any way.

2   I am interested in doing voluntary work and I would particularly like to get involved with your organization.

3   I found out about your organization through researching volunteering jobs [on the Internet/at school/at my local library]. I would like to enquire if you have any opportunities for young volunteers.

How to end a letter

Try ending your letter with something along these lines:

1   I look forward to hearing from you.

2   I would be happy to attend an interview and hope to hear from you soon.

3   I hope that I can be of help to your organization and look forward to receiving your reply.

Practising letter-writing

Have a go at writing a letter to a voluntary organization by filling in the gaps. Each paragraph has already been started.

Dear

I would like to enquire about volunteering opportunities at

I would particularly like to volunteer for your organization because

My interests are

I have not done any voluntary work before, but

Please contact me if there are any suitable opportunities at your organization. I hope to hear from you soon.

Yours sincerely

Dear sir/madam

I found out about your organization through

and I am interested to know if there are any volunteering opportunities which involve

I am   years old and

My hobbies and interests are

I enclose a stamped addressed envelope for your reply and I look forward to hearing from you.

Yours faithfully

Interview tips

It is quite likely that someone at the organization will want to meet you before they offer you a job. If you are asked to go for an interview, don't get in a flap. Simply follow this tried and tested advice.

Do take it seriously and try to look clean and tidy.

Don't turn up looking like you've just staggered out of bed (even if you have).

Do allow plenty of time to get there – the bus is always late when you really need it to be on time.

Don't be nervous – it will be a friendly chat, not an interrogation.

Do be prepared to explain why you chose this organization and how you found out about them.

Do try to appear enthusiastic by asking questions. Here are some questions you could ask:

● What training and support will I be offered?

● Will I be able to claim expenses to cover my transport costs?

● How many other volunteers do you have?

● How many paid staff do you have?

● What will my main duties be?

● How much time am I expected to put in?

● What should I wear?

● Who will be my supervisor?

● Will I get any sort of certification for my volunteering?

● Will I get a reference?

● Will I get the chance to study for an NVQ?

Before you take the plunge...

If an organization wants you to help, that's great. But before you commit yourself, make absolutely sure in your own mind that you want to take on the job. Just because you've contacted the organization or been for an interview doesn't mean you have to accept.

Ask whatever you want to know and find out what you're taking on. Try to talk to volunteers at the organization to get first-hand information. You could ask the volunteer co-ordinator if you can go along sometime to meet the other volunteers and check things out for yourself. If you don't fancy the job after all, try a different organization.

Finally, ask yourself these questions:

● Will I be able to get there and back safely on my own?

● Would I be able to change the arrangements or my level of commitment later on?

● Will I get on with the other people?

● Who will be in charge and with whom will I be working?

● What arrangements are there for support and supervision?

● What health and safety precautions are there?

● Will my volunteering job lead anywhere?

● Does that matter?

If you're happy with all the answers, and your chosen organization is happy with you... good luck with your new volunteering job!

Dos and don'ts

Now that you're a volunteer, here are a few dos and don'ts to help you make the most of your volunteering job.

Do...

...accept volunteer expenses. You can give them back as a donation to the organization if you want.

...stick to any arrangement you have made. If you cannot keep an appointment or are going to be late, let the volunteer organizer know in plenty of time.

Don't...

...overcommit yourself. If you take on too much, you'll only end up letting the organization down.

...leave the project just because you are fed up, having problems or feel you are being taken advantage of. Discuss how you feel with the person in charge of the organization or project first.

...accept money as payment from someone you have helped in the course of volunteering. Explain to them that they can make a donation to the organization if they wish.

...betray any confidences entrusted to you as a volunteer.

Troubleshooting tips

If you have any problems with your volunteering job, first of all go to your supervisor. The chances are that things can be sorted out quickly and easily. Otherwise, try talking to someone else at the organization, such as the volunteer co-ordinator. If you still have problems, get in touch with your local Volunteer Bureau.

You might take on a volunteering job and later decide it's not for you. If this happens, give the organization a ring or write to them to tell them that you don't want to continue. Voluntary organizations are often very busy, so it is important to let them know. If this happens, don't be put off. There are hundreds more exciting opportunities, so just try something different!

Young People's Volunteer Charter

The National Council of Volunteering Opportunities (NCVO) has produced these guidelines to make sure that young volunteers are treated fairly. Every individual has the right to volunteer and as a volunteer you have rights which should be met by the organization. Remember that volunteering is an activity in itself and is not a substitute for paid work.

1. Volunteers should have a clear idea of the tasks they are being asked to undertake, and the responsibility which goes with those tasks.

2. Volunteers should be told who is responsible for their support and supervision. They should have regular contact with this person and the person should ensure that each volunteer is given adequate support.

3. Volunteers should have the opportunity to play a part in the decision-making process of the organization, so that they can represent their own needs and interests.

4. Volunteers should be protected against exploitation and should not be put under moral pressure to undertake work which is against their principles.

5. Volunteers should be adequately protected against any risks involved in volunteering.

6. Volunteers should not suffer financially by volunteering. They should receive all reasonable out-of-pocket expenses.

7. Volunteers should not undertake work which agency staff are being paid to do. Nor should volunteers be used to replace previously paid workers.

8. The relationship between paid workers and volunteers should be complementary and mutually beneficial. Paid workers should be fully aware of the areas of work undertaken by volunteers and the distinction between paid work and volunteering.

9. Young people should be respected under the Equal Opportunities Policy of every organization they may volunteer with.

Whitbread Young Volunteers Awards

Do you know anyone who deserves a pat on the back for the time and effort they put into volunteering? If so, drop a line to the Whitbread Young Volunteers Awards. This scheme recognizes and rewards young people who give up their time to help others, especially those who are ill or elderly, have disabilities or are otherwise disadvantaged.

There are prizes of £1,000 on offer for individual volunteers and for volunteer groups. Each individual winner can spend half the money however they want, and the rest goes to a charity they support. All the winners get to spend a night in London before receiving their awards at a presentation ceremony the next day.

You can find out more and download a nomination form on the web at **www.whitbread-volunteerawards.co.uk**. Or contact them at:

Whitbread Young
Volunteers Awards
Freepost (LOL 1936)
Luton
Bedfordshire LU1 3YR
tel: 01582 397759 or
020 7615 1127

"Volunteering is its own reward. Working for nothing, but paid in full."

Dean Ferrier, Whitbread Young Volunteer of the Year 1996